LAVER

Affirmations
FROM THE
GOLDEN
YEARS

Reflections from the Life of a
BLACK WOMAN MINISTER:
A PARTIAL MEMOIR

outskirts
press

Affirmations from the Golden Years
Reflections from the Life of a Black Woman Minister: A Partial Memoir
All Rights Reserved.
Copyright © 2022 Laverne S. Cathey
v2.0

The opinions expressed in this manuscript are solely the opinions of the author and do not represent the opinions or thoughts of the publisher. The author has represented and warranted full ownership and/or legal right to publish all the materials in this book.

This book may not be reproduced, transmitted, or stored in whole or in part by any means, including graphic, electronic, or mechanical without the express written consent of the publisher except in the case of brief quotations embodied in critical articles and reviews.

Outskirts Press, Inc.
http://www.outskirtspress.com

Paperback ISBN: 978-1-9772-4973-9

Cover Photo © 2022 www.gettyimages.com. All rights reserved - used with permission.

Outskirts Press and the "OP" logo are trademarks belonging to Outskirts Press, Inc.

PRINTED IN THE UNITED STATES OF AMERICA

*This book is dedicated to my children
grandchildren, great grandchildren and
all my "greats" who follow*

Acknowledgements

Anyone who writes a book already knows that it is a long process involving many hours of reflecting, recalling, conversing, writing, and editing. At times it is a lonely process as well. There have been many moments when I had to dig deep inside and face the realities I found there. In order to think, discuss, and write honestly with the hope of producing something that others may find useful requires a "village" of support. I thank God that I have not had to travel this road alone. I am blessed with companions on this journey who have walked with me from the very first handwritten ideas to the final sentences.

First, I want to offer my deepest thanks to Almighty God, who has led me and continues to guide me on this remarkable journey. To my children – Carole, Daryle, Robbie, and Marquel whom I love dearly and whose love and support has been unconditional through the highs and lows of my life.

I would also like to extend my appreciation to my brother, Pastor Rev. Waverly Sanders whose belief in me and my calling into the ministry has been beyond measure. Through him, God has provided resources for my preparation and examination process. He offered pastoral leadership as well as the church community which hosted my

Ordination Service. To my Ordination Committee - Rev. Dr. Luther Ivory, Pastor Rev. Calloway Bain, Minister Elaine Tyler, Minister Edna Sullivan, and the congregation of Channel Hill M.B. Church in Walls, Mississippi. To my brothers and sisters of New Harvest M.B. Church in Memphis, Tennessee where my journey to ordination began. To my Pastor Rev. Glenn Newsom and the Lake Cormorant M.B. Church in Walls, Mississippi for providing a community where I can offer my ministerial gifts in service to God and the Church.

Last but not least, special thanks are due to my writing support team and editors – Associate Editor, Carole Ivory and Senior Editor, Luther Ivory - who have been with me from beginning to end helping me to recall information and communicate it in language that is not only readable but understandable as well. Their belief in the importance of this project and their encouragement motivated me to persevere at times of personal anguish as we labored to bring this project to its completion. Love and Blessings to ALL of you!

Minister Laverne S. Cathey, Memphis, Tennessee October 2021

Table of Contents

Acknowledgements

Preface i

Introduction iv

Affirmations from the Golden Years

Affirmation #1: Prosperity is Our Birthright *Luke 12:32* 3

Affirmation #2: My Personality Is A Manifestation of My Alignment With Divine Principles *John 10:30* 9

Affirmation #3: Faith Inspires Hope in The Midst of Trials And Tribulations *Hebrews 11 & 12* 14

Affirmation #4: Love Keeps Us Connected to God *Romans 8:38-39* 21

Affirmation #5: Love Provides Power for Renewal *Zephaniah 3:17* 27

Affirmation #6: God's Grace Gives Us
   New Sight *2 Corinthians 5:17* 32

Affirmation #7: We Are Connected to the
   Tree Which Helps Us Produce Good
   Fruit *Jeremiah 17; John 15; Galatians 5* 49

Affirmation #8: Seeds We Sow Determine
   the Harvests We Experience *Matthew 13:31-32* 56

Affirmation #9: Tact, Self-Control &
   Humility are Marks of Spiritual `
   Maturity *2 Corinthians 6; Galatians 5* 63

Affirmation #10: Elders of Excellence Are
   Wisdom Carriers *1 Peter 2:9; Acts 1:8* 70

Affirmation #11: The Good News Calls
   Each of Us to Moral Agency *Mark 1:14-15* 77

Affirmation #12: Everyone Needs Guidance
   from Time to Time as We Travel the
   Road Of Life *Isaiah 30:21; 42:16* 86

Preface

Laverne Sanders Cathey accepted her CALL to the ordained ministry in the year 2008 at the age of 70. I wish I had the words to describe the "shock!" that everyone in our extended family network seemed to express upon hearing this news. Not one of us had ever, in our wildest imaginations, thought that she would be standing in front of us announcing her call into the ministry. Even as she struggled to find the words, she did not exhibit the composure that we associated with "standing solidly in one's truth and owning it". We felt that it was "normal" for her to be a bit flustered emotionally, but we were looking to see the "calm" underneath the nervousness. We did not come away convinced.

As far back as I can recall, my mother has never demonstrated any degree of comfortability when speaking publicly. We had seen her as she served the church as an Usher, in the choir as a lead singer, and on the Board of Mothers when she got older. Not one of us could bring our minds to conceive of her serving in the office of ordained ministry. Standing before the family that day, she was behaving as she always had --- nervous, discombobulated, a bit incoherent, and scared. As we tried to associate her with a pulpit ministry of preaching sermons, our image of her standing before us did not square with what she was telling us. It all seemed oxymoronic.

Since that time, our family has been able to witness her growth as an ordained minister of the Word and Sacraments. She has assumed her calling with eagerness and a mind open to learn and to grow in the Office. When I agreed to participate in the publication of this volume as one of the editors of her manuscript, I entered with some hesitancy. However, over this past year I have had a lot of fun assisting her in remembering, relearning, and reliving many of my mother's experiences. We have laughed a lot, cried a lot, experienced both sadness and joy, and given thanks a LOT as we probed her recollections and re-entered her past personal history. She has so many stories that are worth telling. Her life experiences are vast, and now that she has settled into her calling as an ordained minister, she is able to provide frameworks for helping all of us understand what she is thinking and feeling.

This book contains many of my mother's experiences. However, this present volume is not really a memoir in the strictest sense of that term. The stories and examples and explanations that are offered here are all wrapped around her own life experiences, YES! BUT! The main emphasis here is to keep in mind that all the stories, examples, explanations are included to help the reader grasp the CONTENT in each of her AFFIRMATIONS. **Each of the 12 Affirmations in the book aim to promote a perspective that is drawn from her reading and understanding of a particular scriptural text.** Of course, despite the fact that each Affirmation offers a main insight, the "take away" from each Affirmation is still left to the individual reader. I expect that the insights that my mother shares in each of these Affirmations will serve as a springboard for the reader to experience additional revelations. The scholarship and word study found in each Affirmation will be illuminating for those who want to go beyond her offerings here and do further self-study on these transformative biblical texts.

As I look back over my mother's life, I can see clearly how God has guided and protected her. Even during those turbulent times when she wasn't adept at heeding warnings from God OR the guidance of wisdom carriers in her life, God was still there leading her through it all. I am extremely proud of the woman and minister she is now and continues to become.

My mother, along with both of my grandmothers taught me a simple little song when I was a little girl. The song says, "Your mother is a friend that is with you 'til the very end". Today, in my 60s, I know that this is true! And I ALSO know that along with my mother, so is God! May you experience this healing and calming presence of God – and my mother – as you read these Affirmations. Thank you

Carole A. Ivory Associate Editor, LuCar, Inc. Millington, Tennessee Fall 2021

Introduction

The struggle for equal treatment under the law and equity in public policy and cultural norms and mores for women in the United States has been a long and protracted one. White women have been involved in this struggle for centuries as they have navigated a culture characterized by **patriarchal domination and sexist policies and practices** through several "waves" of what scholars refer to as **FEMINISM**. **Feminist thought and practices** have emerged in response to the centuries of sexist and patriarchal practice in the comprehensive culture. Religious communities in America, including the Christian tradition, have been just as blatant in perpetuating sexist practices. In lock step with the broader culture, the majority of these religious communities have also created, encouraged, promoted, and defended the subordination of women throughout the centuries of their existence.

White women who have encountered sexism and misogynist practices in religious communities have also sought to dismantle those structures which have denied them equal access to the resources and leadership in the church. In fact, **the rise of feminist scholarship in religion** can be attributed directly to the continued presence of sexism in religion. Therefore, feminist scholarship in religion can be understood as a direct response to the devaluation of women as humans and the discounting of women's experience as valid for a point of departure in interpreting scripture, constructing theological paradigms, and formulating ethical principles.

Feminist scholarship in religion took its point of departure from **WHITE WOMEN'S EXPERIENCE**. This represents a revolutionary SHIFT in the way leaders of these religious communities had interpreted the authoritative texts and understood the foundational beliefs of their traditions. This also represented an ongoing attempt at **the INCLUSION OF WOMEN'S VOICES** in the efforts to understand, explain, and promote the foundational beliefs of their traditions. White women were challenging the very structures of their religions, arguing that **SEXISM and PATRIARCHY** had **EXCLUDED** their experiences, voices, and talents for centuries throughout the development of their religious communities.

White women's efforts to humanize their religious traditions and excise the sexism from within their ranks was a very noble and badly needed historical project. **Their corrective measures, however, suffered from its own disease ---- White women fell victim to their own racial prejudices and practices.** While recognizing the sexism of white men, white women had an inability to recognize their own racism. Since women's experience was important in religion, where was **the EXPERIENCE OF BLACK WOMEN** in feminist religious scholarship? White women operated under the erroneous assumption that white women's experience adequately represented ALL women's experience.

Black women recognized this error in feminist religious scholarship. Initially, black women began to write as citizens of America, addressing gender issue from black women's perspectives. The realities of racism AND sexism became foundational as points of departure for what was referred to as **WOMANISM OR WOMANIST THOUGHT AND PRACTICE**. Very quickly, class and poverty issues were included as the term **TRIPLE JEOPARDY** was coined by black women (womanist) writers to describe the realities of race, gender, and class oppression that were deeply embedded in black women experience.

Gradually, black women in the religious communities of black people began to analyze, reflect, and write about their religious experiences and perspectives. What these black women faced was similar to what their white sisters faced --- patriarchal domination and sexism in black religious communities. The rise of what is called **WOMANIST RELIGIOUS SCHOLARSHIP** can be understood as a direct response to centuries of devaluing and discounting black women's experiences in black religious traditions. What womanist scholars have sought to do is to identify, name, challenge, unmask, and dismantle sexist, misogynist, discriminating beliefs, policies and practices in black religious communities.

Womanist religious scholarship asserts that black women's experience is a valid resource for interpreting the traditions of black spirituality. Womanist religious thought affirms black women's experience as a much-needed corrective to the one-dimensional understandings promoted through sexism over the centuries. With this emphasis on **BLACK WOMEN'S EXPERIENCE,** womanist thought and practice has provided a "balance" to historic understandings of the faith in the black religious experience.

Laverne S. Cathey's life experiences may be read as a **"WITNESS"** to the ongoing struggles of black women to navigate the sexism of the black church. As a black woman, she has encountered and lived through decades of the "triple jeopardy" of racism, sexism, and classism that has been a feature of black women's experience in America. She has also endured the sexism and patriarchal domination of the black religious community.

In this compelling Volume of Affirmations, as an octogenarian of 83+years of age, Cathey writes as a **COMPANION AND WITNESS to the struggles of countless other black women** who have been victimized by sexist beliefs, policies and practices in the black church for centuries. She relies upon her experiences in the society AND the black church as a black woman to offer insights from her own lifelong quest for dignity and respect. In this way, Cathey belongs to that long tradition of what womanist ethicist Rosetta Ross calls those **"witnessing and testifying" black women** --- Sojourner Truth, Jarena Lee, Fannie Lou Hamer, Victoria Way DeLee and countless others. Like these women before her, Cathey's life represents a demonstration of what womanist scholar Katie Cannon refers to as **"quiet grace" and "unshouted courage"** in her efforts to love and serve the black church.

The reader will be privileged to hear Cathey's own interpretations of scripture, the church, life events, and the human condition. As an **ordained black woman minister in a historically sexist institution (the black church),** Cathey's Affirmations speak her own truth as she continues to embrace the black religious tradition and its churches in love. Cathey is **a daughter of the black church**. She has been nurtured in its bosom throughout her life. This experience allows her to recognize and name its shortcomings and demons while loving its rituals, worship and prayer life, music offerings, social interactions, and opportunities for education. She can appreciate its role in movements for justice in America as well as akcnowledge forthrightly its dismal record relative to women's opportunity and dignity.

As you "enter" into the "world" of these **12 Affirmations (one for each month of the year)**, it is my hope that you will sit at Cathey's feet and drink deeply from the well of one who has lived a rich and varied life. I believe that you will discover deeper insights into your own spiritual experience. I invite you to think of her particular life narrative as a <u>**narrow**</u> window. I invite you to look into that window with focused eyes. In so doing, I believe that previously unrecognized aspects of the **broader** human condition will also be revealed.

Luther d. Ivory Senior Editor, LuCar, Inc. Millington, Tennessee Fall 2021

Affirmations from the Golden Years

AFFIRMATION #1:

Prosperity is Our Birthright
Luke 12:32

It has been called the **Prosperity Gospel**. Sometimes it is referred to as **prosperity theology or the gospel of wealth**. One article I read referred to prosperity gospel as the **religion of capitalism**. Whatever it may be called, it has been a major factor in the way some individual Christians and Christian churches have sought to interpret and promote the NT Gospel of Jesus Christ. This way of understanding the basic meaning of the NT Gospel has been present during the history of Christianity. However, it really seemed to gain a lot of traction in the 1980s & 1990s when several prominent televangelists made it a major feature of their teaching ministries. It took off like a rocket! And although it seems to have waned slightly in terms of its public influence, even now it still carries a great deal of power in the lives of many Christians.

  PROSPERITY is actually one of the central **THEMES** in the Bible. The idea of **SHALOM** in the Hebrew Bible or Old Testament is translated as **PEACE**. However, it has a much deeper meaning in Hebrew. Along with peace, **shalom ALSO means prosperity, wealth, health, and happiness**. When shalom is connected to the Hebrew **words MISHPAT (righteousness, judgement, law) and**

TSEDAKA (righteousness, justice), shalom is expanded to ALSO mean **relationships** that are emotionally, socially, and morally healthy, and which are undergirded by efforts that are loving and just. When prosperity is talked about in the **PROPHETS of the Hebrew Bible or Old Testament**, it takes on the notion of a person or a community that is **IN ALIGNMENT WITH DIVINE PRINCIPLES – IN "RIGHT RELATIONSHIP" WITH GOD!** The prosperous ones are those who treat others with dignity and respect; who take care of those who are most at risk in the society (widows, orphans, outcasts, lepers, poor, etc.); those who use their power and authority for good purposes which benefit and uplift everyone in the community.

In the **NT**, the idea of prosperity ALSO encompasses **much more than economic or financial achievement and success.** This may be why there is a lot of confusion surrounding the so-called "prosperity gospel". The focus on monetary success is what tends to take center position in this type of ministry. It is connected to the idea of wealth, money, land, travel, power, lavish cars and houses, jets and yachts --- the usual **SYMBOLS of achievement in an economy of CAPITALISM.** BUT! The content of prosperity in the Bible actually amounts to much much more than what today's "prosperity gospel" tends to emphasize.

And this is the reason why I had to give this scripture a "double-take", when researching it for this Affirmation. **I discovered that like the promoters of the prosperity gospel, I too had a LIMITED understanding of what PROSPERITY means from a biblical perspective.** Prosperity is more than material wealth. It encompasses a wide range of areas that are not normally considered when we think about prosperity. **The koine' Greek word for prosperity is EVIMERIA. It translates as WELL-BEING, SUCCESS, SAFETY, GOOD HEALTH, MORAL CORRECTNESS, HIGH CROP YIELDS, WISDOM, LONG LIFE, HONOR, and SPIRITUAL GROWTH.** The scope of prosperity is much broader than tangible possessions like money, land, houses, cars, clothes, expensive watches, and other assets. Prosperity ALSO includes things like relationships that encourage, and promote spiritual, emotional, and social health and growth.

AFFIRMATION #1:

In the NT, "evimeria" is often connected to the idea that the SOURCE of a prosperous person or community comes from how well one DISCERNS God's WILL for humanity. Here, prosperity emerges inevitably from the WISDOM a person or community taps into about God's INTENTIONS. In this way, prosperity in the NT ALSO includes a particular kind of KNOWLEDGE – knowledge that leads to wisdom (Sophia)!

The koine' Greek term for knowledge is GNOSIS. Gnosis is much more than facts, figures, or names and dates and ideas. Gnosis is more than intellectual knowledge like chemistry or physics or mathematics. Gnosis is a different type of knowledge. **Gnosis is SALVATIONAL KNOWLEDGE. Gnosis is AWARENESS!!! Gnosis is the type of knowledge or awareness that EMPOWERS, EDIFIES, EQUIPS, BUILDS --- in other words "SAVES"** one from ignorance about what really matters. Gnosis "saves" by providing the believer with an awareness that **COUNTERS ignorance** about what one needs to mature spiritually, emotionally, and relationally – knowledge that **liberates or FREES** us from whatever we are bound to (in ignorance) that keeps us IMMATURE in our development.

Gnosis or saving knowledge has its parallel in the Hebrew Bible or Old Testament term **YADA. Yada translates "to know", to have a deep understanding of".** To "know" something in the YADA sense is to **COMMUNE with it at such a DEEP level of INTIMACY** that it "brings forth" or "procreates". We see the term YADA used in the Creation narrative and other stories in Genesis. "And Adam "knew" Eve, and she conceived and bore.."; "And Abram went in and knew Hagar…"; "And Abraham took another wife Keturah.. and knew her... and she bore…". In these stories, yada or "to know" means **SEXUAL INTIMACY.** YADA means that two people have engaged in a type of UNION or **COMMUNION that PRODUCES** something that is **BEYOND** what was initially there. **TO KNOW someone in a sexual way is to participate in a SACRED ACT.** This is why the very act of sex itself is much more than biological or the mere satisfaction of one's libido. It means that two people come to KNOW each other in a way that is complex, involved, and invested. **I believe that this is the reason why YADA is often connected with the Hebrew word for wisdom -- CHOKMAH.** Using wisdom in sexual engagement means first seeking, recognizing, and then applying intimate knowledge of the other person at a level that **VALUES** that person and **FREES** one from casually using that person as an object to satisfy one's sexual urges.

Gospel writer Luke reminds us that genuine prosperity is NOT merely a byproduct of our discipleship path or faith walk. **Rather, prosperity is our BIRTHRIGHT. A birthright** is a right, privilege, or possession to which a person **is ENTITLED by BIRTH**. Luke promotes the belief that prosperity is actually the disciple's **INHERITANCE**. That is, prosperity is **an ASSET, a BLESSING, a LEGACY** that has been handed down or bequeathed to us simply because we have membership in the household of faith. Prosperity is something to which every believer is **ENTITLED!** Prosperity is something which is passed on to the believer after she or he surrenders to the Lordship of Jeshuah Ha' Meshiah. We don't have to work to EARN it!! **BUT! It is MORE than material property.**

Birthrights? Inheritances? Prosperity? These were the <u>LAST</u> things on my mind growing up in my extended family home in Memphis, Tennessee. But then again, I wasn't aware that God has a way of "dropping knowledge" on little 4-year-old tomboyish girls who are only interested in climbing trees, running through cotton and corn fields, and hanging out with the boys.

God chose my maternal grandmother Emma Stephens to serve as my personal "knowledge dropper". She would pull me away from the boys upon occasion to make sure I learned valuable lessons that girls would need to know. She taught me about angels, key figures in the Bible, along with the important stories in the Bible. She also taught me about the ways in which the Lord was watching over me, and dispatching guardian angels who were constantly protecting me from dangers – both seen and unseen. One lesson she drilled into me was the need to obey the adults in the house. She had me to "KNOW" that my life would be either prosperous or difficult in direct relationship to my

AFFIRMATION #1:

choice to obey those moral rules of conduct that the grandparents and parents had handed down.

As I grew into my early teen years, I began to dismiss these lessons as the talk of old folks who were out of touch with what was really happening. I stopped reading the stories of the Bible. I made up my own moral code and vowed to obey no rules except the ones that I had made for myself. As you might imagine, this was NOT a good decision. I didn't realize how important KNOWLEDGE was in determining one's success or prosperity. When my grandmother would challenge me to be prosperous by committing myself to knowledge that she said would "save" me, I didn't believe strongly enough in her "knowledge" to take it seriously. This approach would land me in serious trouble.

One afternoon at the age of about 13, my grandmother "dropped" another piece of GNOSIS on me. I guess I had seen the boys trying to smoke secretly out back of the smoke house and was trying to follow their conduct. It didn't occur to me that she probably already **"KNEW"** what I was doing and wanted to offer me some gentle correction before anything bad happened. She pulled me aside one day and said, "Young lady, what is done in the dark will soon come to the light. Remember this and you are going to be prosperous in everything you do." Again, I didn't accept this knowledge as "saving" knowledge, so I dismissed it. Her warnings to me were NOT received as YADA or knowledge with which I should be in intimate communion. I still didn't understand the connection she was making between my choices, my conduct, and the prosperous life.

One morning, I decided to obey my own code of conduct, and sneaked into the cotton wagon to smoke a cigarette. You probably already **KNOW** where this is headed. Somehow the match fell out of my hand at the same time that the lighted cigarette embers fell into the tall mound of puffy cotton I had hidden inside. Soon there was a blaze! I learned another piece of YADA and GNOSIS that **morning ---- FIRE AND COTTON DO NOT MIX!** As I hunkered down in my room later that night, ashamed and a bit scared, the saving knowledge that my grandmother had given to me came rushing back into my mind.

A few weeks later, she made a casual remark to me, "young lady, you are going to be prosperous now, I guess, since you aren't going to deal in the dark anymore." She was right. I now have a much clearer understanding of what prosperity really means. It is much more than the accumulation of costly things. A prosperous life is ALSO one that is authentic and open. A prosperous life is **ALSO one that HONORS the KNOWLEDGE** of what is right and what is wrong and tries to consistently **ACT** upon that knowledge. Prosperity is ALSO a life free of moral hypocrisy because it intimately embraces (YADA) saving knowledge (GNOSIS**). My grandmother was a PROSPEROUS woman because she communed with the Divine Principles.** She acted on saving knowledge from the Bible. She once told me that the kind of prosperity that we read about in the Bible was the birthright of all believers. From the day of the cotton wagon fire, I have come to see that she was right.... **Prosperity is our birthright.**

AFFIRMATION #2:

My Personality Is A Manifestation of My Alignment With Divine Principles
John 10:30

"Oh well, I guess we just have to learn to live with her... She's been that way all her life,,,,. That's just the way she is..." How many times have you heard this statement said by a friend or a family member about someone in our circle whose personality traits and behaviors were highly IM-proper and in some cases outright nasty? If your experience is similar to mine, you have heard it a LOT! When I reflect upon this as an octogenarian, I believe that too many of us have used this statement to excuse the ugly, negative behaviors of too many persons. Rather than challenging them to think about the effect of their approach, we have simply let them off the hook so to speak. The result has been that in reality, we have encouraged these persons to continue in their bad behavior rather than challenge them to seek to change it.

What we are dealing with here, in a nutshell, is personality. **Personality is defined as the complex of characteristics that distinguish an individual, a group or a nation.** It is the sum total of an individual's emotional and behavioral traits. Our personality is determined by those qualities, traits, habits of thinking, feeling, and acting which together make up the TOTAL you and me. Put in laypersons terms, **our personality is what comes to people's minds when they are asked to think about us. Our personality is the mental picture, along with those accompanying feelings that people have about us**. Our personalities are what people encounter whenever they interact with us over extended periods of time. And if any of us want to know what our personality IS or is like, all we have to do is ask someone who has known us for some time. They will tell us exactly what personality we are presenting to them.

Personality is a fascinating thing to me. We each perhaps has a notion of what our personality is like, but **since we ALL possess <u>BLIND SPOTS</u> when it comes to understanding ourselves fully**, others' views about US, when honest, can help us to gain insight and clarity about what type of personality we have. This is important to know because our personality is made up of so many traits and characteristics that fit together in dynamic ways. **The end result of all of this is that we EACH somehow, someway manage to arrive at a type of GENERAL way of expressing ourselves or presenting ourselves whenever we are around others over time. This is our personality – how we each come across to other people.**

Some of us are considered to have personalities that are "nice", or "sweet", "stand-off-ish" or "snobbish". Others of us have personalities that are experienced by others as "arrogant" or "narcissistic" or "know-it-all". While others have personalities that are experienced by others as either "helpful", "caring", "compassionate", or "controlling" "divisive", "spiteful", "malicious", "spoiled", "envious", or "malcontented". **The truth is, we ALL have SOME of EACH of these traits or characteristics within us**. The key is how we MATURE over time so that we learn to "check" the UN-desirable traits that cause problems in our relationships with others…. while allowing the DESIRABLE traits of our personalities to GROW and STRENGTHEN. **And while it may be hard to see at first, this has everything to do with HOW WELL WE HAVE ALIGNED OUR PERSONALITY WITH DIVINE PRINCIPLES.**

AFFIRMATION #2:

Like everyone else, I have a personality too. When I reflect upon myself, **I begin to understand more clearly how our personality is SHAPED by those persons, forces, situations, around us --- many of which occur at our earlier times as we grow up in our families of origin.** This is clearly the case with me. I grew up in family where I was the <u>ONLY</u> girl. I had lots of big brothers, and before my teenage years, they tended to treat me as if I was also one of the boys. I had to scrap and fight to hold my own at times when they would try to dominate me. I developed a hard shell over my heart and suppressed my "girlie" sentiments. I became callous and uncaring. Tough and a "take-no-stuff-from-anybody" attitude. I came to feel that I couldn't trust anyone to look out for me but ME!! **End result?? I nurtured a personality that, over time, grew into what most people who knew me identified as a "MEAN LITTLE TOMBOY"!.**

For a very long time, in my relationships with others, I accepted this as the personality that was ME ---- the one that had emerged as the REAL me – the one I was stuck with for life. I acted in ways that perpetuated this personality. I became a spoiled brat. I wanted my own way all the time. I competed with others for time, attention, and favors while believing that I deserved all the great gifts while others were not worthy to be considered. I felt, "This is the way I am, and so people can like it or lump it, but they had better deal with it because this was ME – this was ME! Forever!"

The belief that our personalities are set for life from an early age is NOT one that is compatible with the scriptural focus for this Affirmation. In John 10:30, we are offered a view of life as **a PROCESS rather than an EVENT.** We see the emphasis on <u>**MATURATION and growth**</u> in the life of the disciple who has surrendered to the way of Jeshua Ha' Meshiah. **The message--- the Good News --- from John is that NONE OF US ARE STUCK FOREVER WITH WHO WE WERE OR WHO WE ARE.** Our personalities are NOT fixed or determined by our families or friends. Our personalities are not determined by our enemies or adversaries either. **Who we ARE --- or rather who we WANT TO BECOME is determined ONLY by how willing**

we are to SURRENDER to the Divine Principles set forth in the Gospel of Jesus Christ. When we surrender to God's Principles we are, in reality, <u>**ALIGNING**</u> our beliefs, our thoughts, our attitudes, our commitments, and our actions <u>WITH</u> those Divine Principles.

There are many **Divine Principles which serve as GUIDES** to motivate us to orient our lives in alignment with God's plan for our lives and our relationships ------ reciprocity or the Golden Rule (do unto others as you would have them do unto you); respect for the sacredness, worth, and dignity of others; good manners; a willingness to avoid being judgmental towards others; striving to stress unconditional, redemptive love towards others; ----- ALL of these principles aim to help us to self-reflect, to challenge our own shortcomings and inadequacies --- to experience healing and transformation of our personalities into something that reflects God's love. ALL of these principles direct us toward maturity, compassion, empathy towards others. And… ALL these principles push us to grow and become "peacemakers" who work to establish healthy relationships of love and tact with others. These principles enable us to self-correct.

As we re/focus our personalities to be in ALIGNMENT with these Divine Principles, our personalities will begin to change, to grow, to mature spiritually and emotionally. Our actions towards others will then begin to reflect more of the Divine that is a part of us, and the Ego nature will begin to gradually lose its ability to control our personalities.

As I look back on those early years, I am thankful that God placed other persons in my life who (while I was NOT aware of it) continually presented to me the Divine Principles that I would need to change my spoiled, tomboyish, mean self-serving personality. As I remember, my parents and grandparents ALSO taught me good manners. I was also taught to respect authority. I really didn't know how to work anywhere but in the cotton fields, and I didn't really do a good job at it. Marrying so young, I put my education on hold to go to work to take care of my 3 children. So I needed to develop a good work ethic, and a professional attitude about work.

Eventually I was able to get jobs as a housekeeper and a babysitter.

AFFIRMATION #2:

I started to RECALL the principle of Self-Giving --- "..do your best to clean others' homes as you would your own. Give of yourself to take care of others' children as if they were your own". I began to understand the Divine Principle of stewardship (being a responsible user of my time, talents, possessions, including money). **What had once been BLIND SPOTS to me about my own personality, gradually began to be revealed.** I could see aspects of myself, my personality, more clearly now. I started to pay my bills on time, and I became a person who felt I was NOT being true to God if I did NOT honor my bills enough to pay them. I came to have MORE of a positive view of my self-worth, and saw that all people, including the ones who were my employers were just human beings -- people like me. Eventually, when my oldest daughter had her first child – a son – I was a person with a totally different personality. **I had matured to the point where my personality was so welcoming and compassionate that my grandson began to refer to me by the name "PRECIOUS"!** ---- a very long way from the spoiled, hard, self-centered tomboy of my early years.

John is correct as far as I am concerned. Our personalities, regardless of how they have been --- or are now ---- can be changed, transformed for the better when they are in alignment with Divine Principles. **This is our challenge and our hope --- EACH DAY to focus on our personalities to become MORE and MORE in alignment with Divine Principles ---- and EACH DAY to focus our personalities to become LESS and LESS in alignment with our Ego natures.** This is what Jesus – the Jeshua Ha' Meshiah – means when he says, 'I and my Father are One!" **My Personality Is A Manifestation of My Alignment With Divine Principles.**

AFFIRMATION #3:
Faith Inspires Hope in The Midst of Trials And Tribulations
Hebrews 11 & 12

I love the Church! Without it, my own life would NOT have achieved even half as much as I have been blessed to accomplish. I have 4 beautiful children. I am a grandmother AND a GREAT grandmother. I am a retiree. I have had the pleasure of experiencing the bliss of married life (despite some bad moments too!). As a woman of 83-plus years, I have seen and experienced a lot in life – BOTH positive and not-so-good. Let me say again that I love the Church! It has been the place of refuge and hope during times in my life when I would have given up or been defeated by some difficult circumstances. It just so happens that the place of my heart's love – the Church – has unfortunately, ALSO been the place where I have experienced soul wounds, pain, and disappointments.

My life unfolded in such a way that I received a "CALL" into the ordained pastoral ministry at a late age. I had never expected to be blessed with such an honor. It turned out that the feeling of excitement and eager anticipation about God's call on my life into the ministry gradually gave way to a feeling of betrayal, sadness, dismissal, and negation. You see, I thought that the call into ordained ministry was a

AFFIRMATION #3:

privilege for ANYONE who wanted to serve the church in a particular way using pastoral gifts. However, **I was totally UNAWARE of the ways in which the Church had historically DEVALUED WOMEN in the ordained ministry.** Of all the places that would discount my calling, I never expected the Church where I had worked and served to relegate me and other women to a "place" that forbade us to seek ordained ministry. The church that I loved refused to recognize my call into the ordained ministry as legitimate.

It is a shame and a dishonor to the rich history of women ministers that I was NOT taught anything about these women during my long association with the Church. In fact, I was in my late 70's when I began to hear of names like **Sojourner Truth and Nannie Helen Burroughs**. As I began to hear about **these remarkable women PIONEERS** who preached, testified and witnessed to the glory of God and the truth of the Gospel of Jesus, my hunger to know more about these women grew. I began to read and study more about the journey of Black women religious leaders. I learned about **Jarena Lee, Fannie Lou Hamer, Katie Canon, Delores Williams, and Jacqueline Grant**.

These women, despite sexist beliefs and practices in the Black church, risked their livelihoods, marriages, friendships, and reputations to publicly announce and pursue their calling to preach the Good News. **Many of them had to battle and overcome stiff resistance to enter into the ordained ministry of the Church.** In their undertaking of this journey and struggle, they made important contributions to not only the Church, but the community as well. They preached, taught, and cared for the elderly and sick. They were among the unsung leaders and organizers of the Civil Rights movement in the 1950s – 1960s. They marched, picketed, went to jail, were beaten, arrested, and jailed along with the men like Martin Luther King who were always given the spotlight in the media. There are numerous other women like these whose names and stories are hardly ever mentioned or recognized by the Church that I love.

Even today, when the culture of the Church has opened for the better, there still remains blocks and barriers to accepting and honoring the ordination of WOMEN into pastoral ministry. Women are still denied access to the pastoral office solely on the grounds that they are women. Some churches still will not allow women to sit in pulpits simply because they are women. Women in 2021 are still discouraged from even applying for ordination, excluded from pastoral searches, and are more likely to be discounted in the very few instances when they ARE called to the pastoral office.

I did not expect to encounter such resistance to my calling to the ordained ministry by the Church. Both its pastoral and lay leadership as well as its rank and file membership expressed reluctance about accepting women into the ministry. I was at least aware of the way women were viewed and treated in the culture, on jobs, in the corporate world, in homes, etc. I thought, "Surely these people who are committed to the Church, are disciples of Jeshua Ha' Meshiah, and so they are surrendered to another value system – one based upon love, respect, dignity, and equality." However, I discovered that in too many cases, those values that had been in opposition to the Gospel were, in fact, operating underneath the seemingly loving, warm veneer of church life.

I began to encounter many difficulties when announcing my calling into the ministry. I didn't know about nor understand what patriarchal domination was, nor how sexist notions, customs, and unspoken policies operated in the Church to DIS-EMPOWER women's gifts. There was also a deep-seated misogyny (hatred of women) among a significant core of men in the church that blindsided my efforts to become ordained and left me confused, hurt, and discouraged. **And what surprised me even more, was how thoroughly UN-prepared I was for how many WOMEN IN THE CHURCH were ALSO resistant and dead set against my ordination and the ordination of any woman into pastoral ministry.** Like the sexist men, these women offered numerous, disingenuous excuses for why women were made by God to be second-hand disciples, and therefore should not be granted ordination in the Church.

As I think about this, in my view, it is mind-boggling that **women**

AFFIRMATION #3:

make up 75-85% of the church membership but represent only 3-5% of its leadership. It defies logic and spiritual principles in the Gospel that women can fry chicken in the kitchen, make and serve coffee to the men, run the pastor's aid society, sing in the choir, work the usher board, youth and children's ministries on one hand, but NOT be qualified or embraced to serve in the leadership positions of the Church, on the other hand. **I still wring my hands in confusion as to how black men and women can argue AGAINST RACIAL DISCRIMINATION BY WHITES while at the same time, EXCUSE AND PROMOTE SEXISM IN THE CHURCH BY BLACKS.** If this kind of subordination of women amounts to sexism in the culture, then it ALSO amounts to sexism in the church. ANY belief or practice in the Church that puts others down on the basis of race or color or gender is SIN! It is NOT consistent with the core VALUES and central MESSAGE of the Gospel. **Therefore, sexism (like racism) amounts to an OFFENSE TO THE GOSPEL of Jesus Christ.** And no amount of proof-texting can make it something that God would embrace and promote for God's Church.

I still can hardly imagine all the many ways in which countless other UN-named women of all cultural and ethnic backgrounds whose calling have been and are STILL being continually discounted in the Church. It tends to suck the air out of the room when I think about it. BUT! Into this stifling air comes **a WORD** that opens the window and allows fresh air to breathe. It comes from **the writer to the Hebrew Christians**. This is a book that has a focus that helped to offer me **INSPIRATION and HOPE** as I reflect upon the situation of Black women in the ordained ministry.

The author (attributed to Paul, but there is NO certain evidence to support this claim!) is concerned that the community is in danger of giving way to a sense of despair and defeat. It seems to be **losing its ability to IMAGINE a FUTURE that is BETTER than its Present.** I noticed that the key word for this writer is **"BETTER"!!** This word "better" is used over 7 times from Chapter 7 through Chapter 11. **The word "better" is used to show the difference between the OLD laws** of the community and the NEW law of love through Jesus Christ. The writer is saying "There is a **NEW** sheriff in town, with a **NEW** focus, and a **NEW** plan, a **NEW** way of thinking about life and living, and a **NEW** way of relating to others". "**In the NEW Priest Jesus Christ**", says the writer, "**things are not only NEW, but this NEW is <u>BETTER</u> than the old ways of thinking and being**". When I saw this focus on the NEW and the BETTER, I sat straight up in my chair! I took notice, and I paid attention!

Of course, the HEART of this book is in Chapters 11 and 12. The most quoted verses nearly always come from these two chapters. The message of Chapter 11 is clear. **<u>FAITH</u> is the PATH** which believers must follow in order to achieve **the "BETTER"** that is offered in Jesus Christ. **<u>FAITH</u> means that the believer RE-ORIENTS or ORGANIZES her or his life around the 'BETTER" that is PROMISED by God, but which has NOT been fully seen or manifested.** <u>FAITH</u> means that the believer stakes the totality of her or his life on something that is **NOT YET FULLY EXPERIENCED OR WITNESSED BUT IS HOPED FOR.** And why should anyone live their life on a promise only? "Because…", says the writer, "God, through the person and work of Jesus has promised it, and God's track record speaks for itself". **God ALWAYS DELIVERS ON WHAT GOD HAS PROMISED!**

When I thought about all those women who labored and struggled through hardships to serve as ordained ministers but had NOT been able to experience it themselves or see it achieved by anyone, the writer of Hebrews takes me through a **ROLL CALL OF THE FAITHFUL.** The point? To remind me and others that women who remain true to their call, despite the obstacles they may face, **are NOT LONE RANGERS!** There have been and continue to be others throughout history who BY FAITH have remained true to their calling. The marvelous litany of **FAITH WALKERS** in Hebrews 11 have suffered similar fates as the Black women in the church who have been abused and rejected throughout history in their efforts to become ordained minsters in the pastoral office. These people were despised, abused, and maarginalized. Many suffered horrible treatment. BUT! They kept

AFFIRMATION #3:

on coming!!! They are the **SHOULDERS OF THE FAITHFUL** upon whom we ALL stand, including women who now are in the ordained pastoral ministry. They paved the path for many women like me who were able to hear and follow a call which would lead to challenges which even they could not imagine.

In Chapter 12, the writer **CONNECTS THE DOTS between Divine Promise—Faith---Hope. By remembering the FAITH of those "great cloud of witnesses"** who have paved the way before us, it becomes easier to walk the path of faith ourselves. They believed in God's promises. They kept to the path. They even died in faith NOT having received those promises themselves. **What about us?!** The writer reminds us that although it isn't fair, although it isn't easy, although we get tired --- **IF we stay on the path of FAITH,** we will NOT get so exhausted and frustrated that we will give up and quit. **Faith will ground us in HOPE. HOPE is what produces perseverance through trials and tribulations. Faith is what fuels change because it keeps before us the PROMISES – the "BETTER" that has not yet been seen. Faith never allows us to forget the "BETTER" ... that WE can become.** In this way, faith functions as the key that turns the engine of HOPE. Faith is the "substance" of what these exemplars hoped for, and what we ALL hope for. And faith provides the "evidence" for the BETTER that we can IMAGINE but have not yet seen.

This is what keeps believers going. This is what kept these exemplars of faith going in Hebrews Chapter 11 and 12. **Faith is what kept those legions of preaching women going** who hoped for a chance to serve the church as ordained ministers even though they did not see any evidence that they would one day live to experience it. **Many of these women "died never having received the promise…"** that they looked for and worked towards. And yet, they continued to operate **BY FAITH** in what they had NOT experienced and would NEVER experience. In so doing, **they paved the way for women like me in future years** to be able to experience what they themselves had not, nor never would experience.

What is amazing to me is how God has worked throughout history and in my own lifetime to bring **God's PROMISES** to fruition and completion. Even though the church has many problems which need to be addressed, it can still be used by God in order to bring about God's plans. **Even though the Church remains a sexist community, there are still persons – both men and women – who love and serve the Church as I do, who are working AGAINST sexist beliefs and practices which operate to discriminate against women who have been called by God into ordained pastoral ministry.** These men and women were able to hear and honor God's call to ME in this way, and despite much opposition, these men and women were able to resist pressure to conform to sinful sexist practices. They came together to design and implement a legitimate, Bible-based, Christ-centered, Church-accepted Ordination process and service on my behalf in 2019. Thanks be to them for allowing God to use them in God's work to open the church to **a larger and broader VISION for church leadership that is INCLUSIVE of WOMEN also. As a result of the FAITH of these** persons in the church who strived for the **"BETTER"**, I now serve the Church in the Office of ordained pastoral ministry. **Faith TRULY Inspires Hope In The Midst of Trials and Tribulations.**

AFFIRMATION #4:

Love Keeps Us Connected to God
Romans 8:38-39

Whenever I read this passage of scripture, I never fail to wonder what was motivating Paul to write such life-transforming words. These words reveal a remarkable insight into the nature of God's love and care for humanity: **"For I am convinced that neither death, nor life, nor angels, nor rulers, nor things present, nor things to come, nor powers, nor height, nor depth, nor ANYTHING IN ALL CREATION, will be able to separate us from the <u>LOVE</u> of God in Christ Jesus our Lord."** The words are powerful on their own, but their deeper meaning is very often missed when they are read apart from those verses (vv.18-37) which precede them.

Beginning in verse 18, Paul is acknowledging the reality of sufferings which are a part of human living. Suffering, tragedy, trauma, pain disappointments, and trials, are all very real!! ... and yet, the person who has surrendered to the Lordship of Jesus the Christ, does <u>NOT</u> live her or his life in the shadow of the tragic. The Christian disciple is connected to a deeper, more powerful reality that is able to overcome, heal, and transform situations of suffering, tragedy, and pain into something that is life-affirming rather than life-defeating. This is why Paul can affirm boldly **in this same verse** that sufferings in one's present life, while serious and real, cannot even be compared to the GLORY that is waiting to be revealed in one's future. This is ALSO why Paul can affirm boldly **in verse 28**, that the believer has **a certain knowledge in faith** that **GOD IS IN ALL THINGS, WORKING FOR GOOD** as that person continues to focus on deepening their own love for God and operating with a sense of God's Divine "calling" in her or his life. This is why Paul can FINALLY proclaim boldly **in verse 37** that believers are **MORE than conquerors** over malevolent forces in ALL situations within which we find ourselves living.

What is often missed here is Paul's reasoning for **WHY** he can write such life-transforming words of HOPE and inspiration. Paul points out **in verse 26** that <u>God's Holy Spirit</u> helps to heal us, guide us, intercede for us and sustain us when we are weakened from our sufferings and gripped by hurts and pains, blues and agonies. By the time Paul finishes **verses 31-34**, he has identified the presence of <u>**the entire Trinity – God, Jesus, and Holy Spirit**</u> – as <u>**working on behalf of those of us who are committed in faith to the path of love in Christ**</u>.

Only **AFTER** Paul has acknowledged the **SOURCE** of our ability to cope with and move triumphantly through our sufferings does he make the bold affirmation that <u>**NOTHING is powerful enough to separate us from God's love.**</u> **The word "separate" in New Testament Koine' Greek is "CHORIZO". It translates as divide, pull apart, withdraw, or separate**. It has the same meaning as what happens in a <u>divorce</u> or when someone <u>moves or relocates</u> to another country. Paul is asserting that God's Love is so powerful and certain that we can be assured that <u>NOTHING</u> that happens to us will be able to divorce us from or pull us apart from that love. **Why?** Because God will <u>NEVER</u> leave us or disconnect from us. God will <u>NEVER</u> divorce us nor leave us. This is the essence of the **Divine name <u>EMMANU-EL</u> which translates as "GOD WITH US THROUGHOUT ETERNITY". As far as God is concerned, God has "married" us for life!!! God is never about separation!! God is ONLY interested in UNITING WITH US! In a relationship that is FOR LIFE!!!**

What we often miss is that <u>the **LOVE CONNECTION** we have</u>

AFFIRMATION #4:

with God that cannot be broken……is due to GOD's effort ---- NOT ours!! It all comes from God's side of things. We can <u>NEVER</u> be disconnected from God because God's love will not allow it to happen ---<u>NOT</u> because WE are capable of generating the kind of love that is powerful enough to maintain the love connection on our own. **Paul is clear…. As humans who are limited in ability and power, we simply do NOT possess th kind of power or strength required to make or sustain this "love connection".** We HAVE to rely upon God's power to love US rather than OUR ability to love God. Again, without question, **it comes from God's side of things**.

Paul says to us who may feel disconnected as we live through our hurt and pain, **GOD'S LOVE IS IN ALL THINGS WORKING FOR OUR GOOD** --- even the worst kind of tragedies and sufferings, conflicts and misunderstandings. <u>**God's Love is so strong, so focused, so powerful and sure that NOTHING has the power to DIS-connect US from it!**</u> There is nothing that can happen to us nor anything that we can do that is bad enough to dis-connect us from God's love and care. What Good News!!!! The Christian disciple has the blessed assurance that none of our personal misfortunes nor the negativity that others may plan and implement towards us, will be able to defeat us. Regardless of what we may experience or encounter, our futures remain blessed and assured in the hands of a Loving God who walks with us and cares for us.

We need to hear this word of hope and assurance today, I believe, especially when encountering others who act in ways that may <u>CAUSE</u> us suffering, pain, and trauma. Knowing that God's love is present and actively working in such situations for GOOD will keep us grounded in God's Love. This will, in turn, enable us to choose to be **CO-WORKERS with God** in the situation. Only then will we be able to offer life-affirming words and actions that demonstrate the therapeutic Love of God which is operating in and through us to heal.

I had not arrived at THIS place of understanding in my own faith journey at the time of my marriage of 17 years. So, I wasn't able to see the truth of Paul's bold claim about God's love. Perhaps I had married too young (I married at the VERY young age of 16). Further, I came from a family of 6 boys and only 1 girl (ME!). So perhaps I was a little too spoiled at the time. Then I ended up married to a man who was also spoiled and emotionally immature. He was NOT yet ready to be a responsible man nor a supportive husband. And this combination of our personal hang-ups, and lack of a clear faith path led to my enduring a marital union that was beset with mistrust, conflict, pain, abuse/violence and isolation. As a result, I suffered as a battered wife for most of married life.

Eventually through the help of friends, I reconnected to church life. I began to attend Sunday School and worship every Sunday. I had heard about God, Jesus, and faith. I knew the stories of the Bible. BUT! In reality, I really did not KNOW God at a deep, personal level and so I was not experiencing the love of God that Paul talks about. Further, **I could not grasp the notion of God's love for me because I had buried myself so deep in my own pain until I could ONLY hear about God's love THROUGH my pain.** My ears had become plugged and my heart had become closed. Therefore, **I could NOT really HEAR nor ACCEPT God's love.** I was too beat up and abused and traumatized.

As I continued to GROW IN FAITH, I began to mature spiritually and gradually I was able to discern that what I was going through and enduring in my marriage, as painful as it was, was somehow, someway connected to God's love. As I began to emerge from my own fogginess and numbness, I started to gain my "faith eyes". I realized that while I didn't know it at the time, **God's love was always there with me** – sustaining me, guiding me, encouraging me, healing me, strengthening me – to help me make the decisions that were worthy of me and the positive value God had placed on my life. Even while I was being abused and battered, God still continued to love me and remain connected to me. God placed in my path many other women who had experienced abuse, as well as men who were living out God's love in their relationships. Through these remarkable persons and my own

AFFIRMATION #4:

efforts, I saw a manifested demonstration of the ways God's love keeps us connected despite OUR weaknesses and experiences of suffering.

I see now that it was God's power and ability to love me that kept me connected to God---- <u>NOT</u> the other way around! In actuality, because I was so consumed with just surviving the abuse, I had very little genuine love to offer anyone – including myself. And yet, because God was faithful to ME through God's love, I was NEVER DIS-connected from God. And so, I was able to gradually generate enough genuine love so that something beautiful resulted --- 4 lovely children (2 daughters and 2 sons!) --- **ALL THROUGH GOD'S LOVE OPERATING IN A SITUATION OF TRAUMA, LOVELESSNESS, PAIN, AND ABUSE.** God was working in that experience to keep me connected to God. God's love was working towards a positive outcome – for ALL our good, even when we were not aware of it.

Even when other persons exhibit personality traits, habits of character, and actions that are <u>not-so-loveable</u>, **God's Love** keeps us connected to their humanity. It is **LOVE** that will <u>NOT</u> allow us to fail to recognize the **VALUE** that God has placed in them. Love reminds each of us that even those who we may feel are the "least deserving" of our love and care are still made in the **Image of God**. It is that **Divine Imprint** in each of us that makes us <u>**persons whose lives are sacred and of inestimable value and worth, deserving of dignity and respect**</u>. It is Love at work in us that enables us to continue to find ways to recognize, affirm, and enhance VALUE in each of us.

None of us are fully what we <u>ought</u> to be, but we can take comfort in knowing that no genuine seekers on the path of love are what we <u>used</u> to be either... and thanks be to God, none of us are what we are <u>going</u> to become. <u>**We are all works in progress, and only LOVE can create, recognize, and enhance value in our own life and the lives of others**</u>. If we want to remain connected with God, it must be **though love, NOT around it**!

I John 4:7-21 reminds us that **God IS LOVE**... and those who claim to be seekers of the Christ must demonstrate that connection through relationships based upon that love. This is what Jesus directs genuine seekers to accept as an ethical challenge in **John 13:34-35: "As I have loved you, so you must love one another. By this everyone will know that you are my disciples, if you love one another"**. Paul reminds us that God's Love connects us to God and to each other, and provides victory over all situations we may encounter in life. **Love Keeps Us Connected To God.**

AFFIRMATION #5:
Love Provides Power for Renewal
Zephaniah 3:17

My daughter loves plants. She enjoys talking to them and showing them special care daily. While all her plants have their own uniqueness, none of them are more spectacular than the beautiful **TROPICAL HIBISCUS** that sits on her back patio. When it comes into full bloom, its radiance is unmatched. It lights up her flower garden with such splendor that her neighbor comes by just to gaze at it along with all of us. The only problem with the tropical hibiscus is that each of its individual flowers bloom for only ONE day. Then the flower withers and falls to the ground, to bloom no more!

Since my daughter lives in an area of town that has beautiful, lush trees and other vegetation, her place also serves as home to many other unique life forms as well. One day a beautiful bright green **LUNA MOTH** flew in and landed on her porch. Its large wings were shades of green and yellow. It sat in place for several days. One morning, after about a week, the moth suddenly flew off the porch, performed several aerial dips and dives, and landed on its side on the deck. It then flipped itself onto its back, fluttered briefly, lay still, and died immediately!

For all of their scintillating color and beauty, the tropical hibiscus blooms for a day, and the luna moth struts for a week. Then like a flash

– its over! Their lives come to an abrupt end. We are left to ponder how something so visually stunning can be so fleeting and short-lived. What lessons can the hibiscus and the moth teach us about our own lives?

The Prophet Zephaniah shares a portrait of God's love and care that runs <u>counter</u> to the experience of the tropical hibiscus and the luna moth. Writing to the nation at a time when Israel had returned from Babylonian Exile, Zephaniah witnessed the sheer exhaustion of a people who had just gained their freedom. They were preoccupied with their own affairs and rebuilding and beautifying their own dwellings. This left them little time for anything else that was meaningful. The task of rebuilding the Temple (the Lord's House) which lay in ruins, was neglected. This important work had ceased for years. Zephaniah observed this and became alarmed! He delivered the message that although the people were tired and exhausted, they would be given renewed strength as they relied upon God.

Zephaniah reminds Israel and all of us that God's love is empowering for those who commune in it. **"…He will renew you in His love…"**. Unlike the short, limited span of life that nature's blueprint has determined for the tropical hibiscus and the luna moth, God's love and care has provided a way of continually reviving the human spirit.

I am sure that all of us can recall times in our lives where we have radiated with splendor in the work we have done or in the results our presence has manifested. And yet, no matter how grand or spectacular our achievements may have been, they are all short lived, limited, and eventually forgotten. Further, the commitment to put forth these efforts, requires such vast amounts of energy that we are often left fatigued and exhausted. We soon need more energy to power us to keep on going. **"…He will renew you in His love…"**.

When I feel tired and weary… when I feel my energy depleted… when I feel as if I have given all I have and cannot summon anything more to display…, the words of the Prophet Zephaniah direct me towards the Source which can and will replenish my spirit and give me a new zest for life. **God's abiding LOVE will refresh, recharge, and**

AFFIRMATION #5:

renew me. I can turn and rely upon God's love. In that communion with God, I don't have to shine with great pomp or splendor for a little while, and then retreat to a place of lackluster living. I don't ever have to view my life as a tropical hibiscus or a luna moth --- beautiful, splendid, short lived – a big "bang" and then nothing more to give! **"…He will renew you in His love…"**.

I can recall a point in my life where I needed God's renewing energy. I was in the middle years of my 17-year marriage. My husband was not providing the emotional, physical, spiritual, or economic resources that I and my children required to keep the family healthy and running smoothly. I didn't really know how to provide these resources either at a level that was optimal, especially on the economic level. I DID know how to pray though, and I held to the belief that God would always answer my prayers.

One day, I went to the pantry and there was no food on any of the shelves. Nothing! My hungry children looked at these bare shelves, and with concerned looks on their faces asked me, "Momma what are we going to eat today?" My response to them? "Only God knows!" This was hardly an acceptable answer from a mother to her hungry children, and I can still feel the emotional weight of disappointing them as I looked at their faces. There had been too many times when I remembered taking my children to church without breakfast. Or lunch….

As I sat on the living room couch emotionally depleted, tired from trying unsuccessfully to figure it all out without help from my husband, I wrung my hands. I was at the end of my powers to cope, or problem-solve. In truth, I was giving up. I sat there in a daze, feeling sorry and not knowing what to do – when suddenly like a rock out of the blue, there was a rude knock at the front door. I knew that knock! I had heard it many times before, and when it came the way it came that morning, it was <u>NOT</u> a welcome sound. It was my uncle. A weekend drunk who always managed to find my house when he had run out of liquor and money and needed a place to sleep it all off.

I was NOT in the mood for him nor his alcohol-addicted personality that morning. I opened the door, let him in, and set myself to give him the full force of my anger. But, before I could get a word out, my uncle (who was notorious for his lack of financial responsibility! Who NEVER had any money!) came in SOBER! For once, he was in his right mind! He said, "Hey honey…, I'm going to head to the grocery store to buy you and these children some food to eat." I was shocked! Stunned! In a daze actually! I smiled and thought 'Aw shucks! What a blessing from God!". I knew this had to be God working through my uncle to provide resources, and energy to cope. I felt my spirit being renewed. I felt my strength returning.

This points to the therapeutic effect of God's love and care. God's love is healing, empowering, sustaining, and renewing. It works to revive the exhausted spirit and give hope to the despairing heart. God's love is expressed through God's Self-giving on behalf of others. **John 3:16** says that **God loved the world in such a way that God GAVE God's Self so that those who believed would receive the GIFT of eternal LIFE. Because of God's love and care for us, everything God does in every situation is ultimately LIFE-GIVING, and RENEWING. "…He will renew you in His love…".** God's love is always working to renew us and empower us -- sometimes through the work of others like my uncle – persons we may LEAST expect to exhibit God's love. OR… Sometimes it is through persons like my grandmother who babysat my children and taught them (and me) about the love and care of God. Not only did she teach us the stories of the Bible, but she also performed loving acts of giving (money, food, clothes, rides…) to help us make it. We can count on God's love and care to send those Good Samaritans our way just at the time we are most in need. In this way, WE can expect to become Good Samaritans ourselves at some point in our lives, participating in God's work of renewal.

For us, the renewing power of God's love enables those who commune with it to offer that same love and care to others who also may be faltering on life's journey. As people experience pain, suffering, despair, and become fatigued with just trying to survive on a daily basis, the love of God operating in the human heart revives the spirit. It empowers the weary spirit to recover and recapture its vigor. It gives nourishment

AFFIRMATION #5:

for sharing that same love to and with others. As Paul' says to us in **I Corinthians 13 God's love, "bears…believes…hopes…and endures…all things. It NEVER fails."**.

I challenge each of us to make time to commune daily with God's Love. It will revitalize our spirits and give us renewed strength each day. "**…He will renew you in His love…**". **Love Provides Power for Renewal.**

AFFIRMATION #6:
God's Grace Gives Us New Sight
2 Corinthians 5:17

When I went to visit my **optometrist** to get fitted for glasses, I was diagnosed with astigmatism and early glaucoma issues; I was fitted for glasses and wore them with some improvement of my eyesight; However, they did not fully achieve what the optometrist was aiming for, and my eyes required further treatment; the Dr gave me some eyedrops to address the glaucoma issue. She hoped that the drops would assist the eyeglasses to restore my eyesight to near-20/20 vision. Well…. I can share with you now that unbeknownst to my eye doctor, **I NEVER USED THE EYEDROPS THAT SHE PRESCRIBED FOR MY CATARACT PROBLEM.** When I returned to the optometrist office 14 months later, my Dr asked me how I liked the eyedrops; I laughed and avoided even responding. I didn't want to lie to her, so I said nothing. She said, "Well you will probably need some more of these eyedrops since it has been over a year, and they worked so well for you". I didn't use the drops for the purpose that they were intended, so I never knew whether they were effective in helping my eyeglasses to correct my eye problem.

Today, I still wear corrective eye lenses, but I do not enjoy 20/20 vision. I still require additional measures to see when I am driving or

AFFIRMATION #6:

reading or watching television. I still experience some glaucoma issues. I often wonder would I have benefitted from using those eyedrops... oh well, I guess I will never know…

Like me, there are millions of people in the world who suffer from numerous eye problems and eye diseases which act as barriers to our ability to see with 20/20 vision. You could probably name about 5 of these without even blinking if you had to… What comes to mind? amblyopia, retinitis, dyslexia, dry eye, myopia, etc. Since my diagnosis and treatment in 1980, ophthalmologists and optometrists work with advanced eye technology, and there are probably even more eye problems identified along with more ways of addressing those problems. Today, we can even have Lasix surgery to "correct" faulty sight; we've come a long way, baby!

As I reflect on this aspect of my life, I now **SEE** this experience through a theological lens, if you will. I am reminded of the powerful 13th Century Hymn of Prayer by Richard of Chichester. It is a plea for the disciple to experience daily spiritual growth and deeper faith --- **in a word MATURITY**. And the notion of **spiritual sight or IN-sight is part of that growth process:**

Day by day, Dear Lord; Of Thee three things I pray. **To SEE Thee more clearly.** To love Thee more dearly. To follow Thee more nearly. Day by day.

As I meditate upon these words as an ordained minister of the Christian Gospel, **I am led to wonder how it is with our SPIRITUAL SIGHT these days in 2021?**

What I was completely **UN-aware** of during all my years of church membership as a Christian disciple, was how often the concepts relating to **SIGHT or SEEING, EYESIGHT, AND INSIGHT** are mentioned in the Bible. **In the Old Testament alone, "eye" and "eyes"** are mentioned <u>over 63 times</u>; **"sight"** is mentioned <u>once</u>; **"see"** is mentioned <u>10 times</u>. If we consider the words that relate to **the act of "looking" (look, looketh, looked)**, we can identify <u>over 30 instances</u> in the Old Testament alone.

In the New Testament, "eye" and "eyes" are mentioned <u>over 21</u>

times; **"see"** is mentioned <u>over 20 times</u>; **"sight"** is referenced at least <u>3 times</u>. And again, if we add into the mix those words associated with **"looking" (look, looketh, looked)**, we find <u>over 11 instances</u> in the New Testament. So the sheer number of times that stories and examples related to sight and seeing are highlighted in the Bible speaks to just how important this concept is to proclaiming God's liberating work in the world.

In fact, in three of the most memorable and widely referenced public healing narratives in Matthew 21, Mark 10, Luke 18, **Jesus RESTORES the eyesight of four blind men**. In so doing, Jesus demonstrates the way in **which AWARENESS of God's RE-making of the world occurs gradually over time.** Here, we are invited to **"SEE"** the ways in which God RE-FORMS the life of the believer. God does this by **empowering believers to become delivered from SPIRITUAL BLINDNESS and to become increasingly more AWARE of and CONSCIOUS of God's VISION for a NEW WORLD.**

And again, as we RE-learn in the remarkable account of **Jesus' healing and restoring of sight to the blind man in Mark 8:22-26,** the disciple cannot access this NEW world by observation with physical eyesight. Rather, **the believer is given NEW EYES with which to SEE all of reality in a different way, on a different plane, from a different perspective using a different set of values and virtues. In other words, believers are given a NEW PARADIGM by which to SEE or DISCERN what God is up to in the world – the NEW THING God is doing in our midst.** This is what **INSIGHT or NEW SIGHT** means in the New Testament public teachings and healings of Jesus ---- **the capacity to SEE what is OLD through NEW LENSES** and thereby **DISCERN or become AWARE** of what is really TRUE, RIGHT, VALUABLE, GOOD, AND JUST.

All of this is a very big deal for the Apostle Paul. In his 2nd Letter to the Church at Corinth, Paul writes what turns out to be his most personal Letter. In fact, BOTH of Paul's Letters to the Church at Corinth are written to a community which Paul himself had founded on his 2nd missionary journey. **The church had become infected with various**

AFFIRMATION #6:

"tendencies" which worked against their ability to continue to CLEARLY SEE or CLEARLY UNDERSTAND their PURPOSE as a community of faith. The tendency to flaunt eloquence and oratory; the tendency to become infatuated with philosophical concepts and Greek myths; the tendency to discredit Paul's ministry and viewpoints – all these had led to schisms and the formation of different factions and parties in the church. The unity of love had been broken and the church had to RE-orient and set itself on a different path.

What Paul knew is that **NO positive change can occur in a person or a community with-OUT the capacity to SEE the VISION of something NEW and different. What had been lost at Corinth was the capacity to SEE or DISCERN God's intentions for the community.** So they floundered aimlessly. They got caught off-track with pointless ideas and rituals. They had lost their direction, and the ONLY remedy for lost direction is the ability to **SEE** a NEW PATH.

So Paul begins working on their **EYES** by appealing to their hearts. He offers tender love as he focuses upon his motives. He is aware that there is an element in this church which has been focused on discrediting his ministry and authority. So, he shares with them his spiritual passion for his ministry. If he can get them to **SEE** his intentions with **NEW EYES**, then he knows they can regain their own spiritual direction and **REFOCUS** their own ministry. Their spiritual eyesight will be corrected, and new sight can occur.

Paul reminds us that **Grace (in Koine' Greek, the word is "CHARIS" which means Unmerited, Undeserved favor or Unearned gift)…..** is THE corrective for our faulty spiritual sight. **God's GRACE gives us new sight AND insight.** This is a spiritual sight. It amounts to **an AWARENESS of the presence of God.** God is already present with us, but we are not always aware of it. This new sight which grace provides, gives us **the capacity to SEE BEYOND the natural or physical eye, and to discern or to be aware of God's working** at many levels which are much deeper and broader than can be detected with the natural eye. We are able to **SEE** and understand that even in difficult, tragic, painful, life-threatening situations, God IS at work IN us, THROUGH us, AROUND us and OTHERS.

We are able to see the way that the Prophet Elisha's EYES saw God's army of protection around him while on a dangerous journey in 2nd Kings Chapter 6. Elisha's attendant was worried and fretful because he knew there was a huge Syrian army waiting to capture and possibly kill them. Elisha prayed that this young man's **EYES** would be **OPENED.** When God opened the young man's eyes, he could **SEE** what Elisha had SEEN all along with **the eyes of faith.** He saw a mountain full of horses and chariots of fire surrounding him and Elisha, waiting to protect them. This is what it means to have **NEW SIGHT - an awareness of God and God's presence with us.**

And this **new awareness** is not only about THEM out there….. It is ALSO about the ME in here! It is an inside job! Since it is by Grace that we are **SAVED (Koine' Greek word is "SOZO" or "SOTERIOS" which means rescued or delivered),** we are now able to **SEE** the TRUTH about ourselves more clearly. We are rescued from the false illusions we harbor and nurture about ourselves. In turn, We can **SEE** more clearly what is happening around us, WHY it is happening, and what we might do to help make things better. In this way, **Grace "SAVES" us by operating in our lives to give us more HIND-sight, IN-sight and FORE-sight.** Our dim sight is gradually corrected to 20/20 spiritual vision.

And Paul doesn't stop there! He retrieves a point he has made in the **13th Chapter of his 1st Letter** to the church at Corinth. He says that **while we remain in this world, even with a NEW and IMPROVED Spiritual Sight, our "EYES" still won't operate at our highest level of "seeing".** We will still "see" or "discern" events and experiences as if we were looking at an image of ourselves in a room that is dimly lit. Only in God's consummation of history will we **FULLY and COMPLETELY "SEE"** or **"KNOW"** or **"UNDERSTAND"** what God has been up to in the world and in our own lives all along.

And yet, as Paul boldly claims in **verses 16-18 of 2nd Corinthians, Chapter 5**… whatever we are experiencing at any given moment may cause us grave concern and may even confuse us… BUT! It will never

AFFIRMATION #6:

distress us, lead us to despair nor destroy us. Why? Because we have been given **NEW EYES - NEW SPRITUAL EYES** - by which to **SEE** what others may never see – the hand of God at work in that situation. Others may see catastrophe and afflictions. **WE SEE what is NOT seen… with the eyes of faith**. We see the presence of God working through ALL things to bring them to the purposes for which God has intended. And so, we are actually **RE-NEWED** in our faith through our capacity to **SEE** the **UNSEEN** by what Paul refers to as **God's ABUNDANT GRACE**.

This is so clearly seen in the life of a man who wrote one of the most beloved hymns in the Christian tradition. Over 249 years ago, **the English slave trader John Newton**, experienced this saving Grace. In his early life, Newton thumbed his nose at the notion of God. He mocked the idea that religious conversion was genuine. While on a sea voyage transporting slaves from Africa in 1748, Newton's ship was caught in a violent storm. In this life-threatening, near-death experience, a crew member who had replaced him on the deck of the ship was thrown overboard into the waves and drowned. Newton experienced a sudden conversion of the heart – a genuine spiritual awakening – and began to pray for the safety of his crew and ship. The ship and crew survived the storm, and Newton now had a newfound faith. **BUT! Newton's EYES still had NOT yet received the NEW SIGHT that God's Grace was offering to him**. So he continued to work in the inhumane, immoral slave trade – **blind** to its injustices.

In 1754, Newton retired from the business of slave trading, accepted a call from God, and was ordained into the Christian ministry in 1764. In 1772 at the age of 47, Newton began writing a hymn that would gain universal acceptance and popularity as a witness to the **"Grace"** that had saved him from a life of wretchedness and moral callousness. What is remarkable about the hymn is the ways in which Newton continuously asserts to the listeners that **it was God who found HIM, NOT the other way around. HE was a wretch. HE was lost in his sin. He WAS BLIND!!!! GOD FOUND HIM!! GOD'S GRACE OPENED NEWTON'S EYES…and changed him…SAVED him…**

Newton eventually became an anti-slavery advocate, and worked tirelessly for the abolition of the slave trade.

Newton penned the following words in the Hymn we now know as **"Amazing Grace"** as a witness to his own deliverance:

"Amazing Grace, how sweet the sound… that saved a wretch like me; I once was lost but now I'm found… **was BLIND but now I SEE…**"

Thanks be to God…for the <u>New Sight</u> that God's Amazing <u>Grace</u> Gives to All Believers.

Me at Age 16

Me with my "nuclear" family -- the Sanders
(front row, left to right) = brother Earl, father Mose, mother Katherine, and ME;
(top row, left to right) = brothers Waverly, Barry, WillieRoy, Hadarii, and Michael

Me in my late '30s as a new divorcee in Memphis, Tennessee. This picture marks an important period in my life. It is the beginning stages of a discernment about the call to a more serious spiritual engagement. Although I did not know it at the time, my response would set me on a journey that would eventually lead to my ordination into the Christian ministry as a preacher and teacher of the Gospel.

My children (left to right) = Daughter Robbie, Son Daryle, youngest son Marquel, and daughter Carole

Me with Family at Gathering @ Wyndham Resorts in Nashville, TN in 2017;

My ONLY granddaughter Candice, her husband Paul, and grandtwins Nia and Ellis. Like me, Candice is the only "grandgirl" born to my "line" in her generation. She inherits the "mantle" of carrying this reality. It can be a "burden" at times, but the love of God shines through her life. She is truly a genuine "gift" from God!

Me, with my brother Rev. Waverly Sanders and his wife Tonia after worship at Lake Cormorant Baptist Church in Walls, Mississippi in October 2021

Certificate of License

This Certifies That

LaVerne S. Cathey

having given evidence of the call of God to

The Gospel Ministry

is licensed to preach the Gospel, perform marriages, administer the Sacraments, and to direct the other functions of the Ministry.

And is hereby awarded this Certificate by

New Harvest M. B. Church
Organization

Memphis, Tenn.
City and State

on this **7th** day of **April** year **2010**

Raymond Tucker
Witness

Kenneth Lee Pinkney
Pastor

My Certificate of License to Preach, Awarded by my then-Pastor Kenneth L. Pinkney and Deacon Board Chair Raymond Tucker, at New Harvest Baptist Church, Memphis, Tenessee April 2010

Certificate of Ordination

This Certifies That

Lavern Cathey

has completed all the requirements for ordination as a minister of the Gospel of Jesus Christ and is hereby commissioned to teach the Word, preach the Gospel, and to administer all the sacraments, ordinances and other functions of the church,

And is hereby awarded the certificate

by

Channell Hill M.B. Church
Organization

Walls, MS
City and State

on this _13th_ day of _May_ year _2018_

Waverly Sanders   _Rev. Dr. Luther Ivory_
                     Committee Chairperson

FINALLY! My Certificate of Ordination Awarded at Channel Hill Baptist Church, Walls, Mississippi on May 2010. Signed by my Pastor (and brother) Waverly Sanders and the Chair of my Ordination Committee Rev. Dr. Luther Ivory.

Me, in October 2021 wearing the clergy collar after my ordination into the Christian ministry.

AFFIRMATION #7:

We Are Connected to the Tree Which Helps Us Produce Good Fruit

Jeremiah 17; John 15; Galatians 5

As you may recall from some of my earlier Chapters in this book, I was raised in a farming family. My father was a sharecropper who planted all kinds of things – cotton, beans, greens, corn, to name a few. Farming put our family in a rustic environment where there were lots of trees, vines, shrubs, and bushes around everywhere. Being the tomboyish girl that I was, I ran with my brothers, and got in as much mischief as they did, trying to keep up with them and do all the things they did. **Two of our favorite activities was climbing <u>TREES</u> and "riding" <u>VINES</u>.**

My brothers and I would climb any <u>**tree**</u> that we felt was a challenge. We would race to the top of <u>**trees**</u> so tall that we would have died before we landed on the ground had we fallen. This gave my mother so much anxiety and fear that she forbade us to climb. Eventually we discovered another form of fun that was much closer to the ground. We called it riding the **<u>VINES!</u>** On our land was several **<u>vines</u>** that were so strong that they could support our weight. We would climb them and swing from one **vine** to the next, gradually moving from place to place without ever touching the ground.

Thankfully, we were all fortunate to never fall from a **tree** nor a **vine**. I remember how much fun we had climbing and "riding". BUT! I never paid much attention to the **TREES or VINES** that served as the source of so much enjoyment. I don't think I ever thought much about the purpose of some of the <u>trees</u> that we climbed – like **mulberry, apple, peach, and oak trees**. And I didn't think much about how the <u>vines</u> we "rode" – like **grape, fig, and elderberry vines** – provided a source of food and nourishment for our family to eat. The **TREES and VINES** served a purpose beyond our childhood enjoyment. They were important for our family's livelihood.

There is a saying down South that goes like this: **"You don't know how you look… 'til you get your picture took!"** John, the Apostle, Son of Zebedee, the "Beloved Disciple" of Jesus, seems to have heard and adopted this approach to ALL his New Testament writings. In addition to the Gospel of John and the apocryphal book of Revelations, he wrote the Letters of I, II, and III John. His writings are highly influential in the New Testament canon. In fact, only the Apostle Paul has more books included in the New Testament. In ALL of his writings John uses **METAPHORS and THEMES** like love, hospitality, and service to **strengthen the faith of believers**. John ALSO uses **"PORTRAITS" or PICTURES"** that describe the character and work of Jesus the Christ. John took Jesus' <u>picture</u> so that we could really see how Jesus looks.

In the Gospel of John, there are 21 Chapters, and John employs a different <u>**PORTRAIT**</u> of Jesus in <u>**EACH**</u> of them **to inspire faith in Jesus as the Son of God**. John is a creative writer with an active imagination. This allows him the ability to use <u>**"portraits"**</u> or <u>**"metaphors"**</u> like bread, water, servant, king, teacher, conqueror, defender of the weak, restorer, physician, shepherd, and intercessor to emphasize some special aspect of Jesus the Christ. **Unlike me in my childhood and teenage years, the Apostle understood and appreciated the importance and value of the <u>trees and vines</u> in the areas where he lived. In Chapter 15, John "paints" a "portrait" of Jesus as the "TRUE**

AFFIRMATION #7:

VINE". The point of this "picture" is to declare that among all the aspects that Jesus possesses as the Savior, **Jesus is ALSO the SOURCE OF ALL SPIRITUAL "FRUIT"**.

Here, John uses the metaphor or picture of a **VINE** to describe **the UNION** between **Christ** and the **Church**. What is true for the Church is ALSO true for the **individual believer**. The metaphor of **VINE (the Koine' Greek word is AMPELOS)** provides a concrete visual object for John to explain a profound spiritual reality. Of course, for a culture whose very survival is dependent upon grapes, olives, figs, and pomegranates, John's choice of images here is easy to understand. Each of these staples is produced by a **VINE** (sometimes translated as small BUSH or small TREE). **The VINE functions as the MAIN CHORD of life. The VINE contains the ROOTS that are attached to the ground and the water supply** from which valuable, life-sustaining nutrients are found. Grapes, olives, figs, lemons, pomegranates are all nourished by a **VINE**. This is why the care of **VINEYARDS** is so important in the culture of John and Jesus.

Fruit cannot grow if the branches to which they are attached have been severed from the **VINE.** John uses the **Greek word CHORIZO** to describe the experience of being **cut away or detached or separated**. It means that there is **NO connection.. NO communication.. NO exchange of energy... NO give and take** between two things or people. When the **branches of the vine** are connected, at a deep level there is an exchange of energy and information that takes place. John uses the **Greek word MENO** to describe **a state of MUTUAL giving and receiving**. "Meno" means a **CONTINUOUS, UN-INTERRUPTED state** of living, residing, dwelling in the company of someone, some group, or some community.

And yet, **"Meno" suggests another DEEPER LEVEL of RELATIONSHIP**. 'The closest English word for **"meno"** is **"SYMBIOSIS. Symbosis is a term used in biology to describe a long-term interaction between two different organisms that live in close physical association to the advantage of both.** Two people or organisms in symbiosis are called **SYMBIONTS**. **Symbionts, DWELL TOGETHER and INTERACT WITH and ACCEPT what each other gives without resistance or protest.** WHY? Because each person or organism **NEEDS or REQUIRES precisely what the other provides.** What each organism or person provides is something that is <u>absolutely necessary for the other's survival</u>…. BUT!!..NEITHER person or organism is able to provide that necessity for itself.

The way that symbiosis works can be seen immediately in the case of two organism that grow in the forest or on trees in your yard – <u>lichens and algae.</u> **Lichens are made up of fungi** that live in a symbiotic relationship with algae. **Algae are green plants** that make their own food through a process called photosynthesis. **Fungi like lichens do NOT make their own food.** They have to get nourishment through a food supply that is provided by something else – namely algae. The algae needs water. However, **algae are NOT able to make their own water**. They have to get their water supply from another source – namely fungi. Lichens are fungi. **So lichens and algae live in a symbiotic relationship as symbionts, mutually benefitting from the interaction between each other**. Lichens furnish the water. Algae furnish the food. Both contribute to the survival of the other, while neither could survive on its own. This is what symbiosis between 2 symbionts looks like. This is what John is describing when he uses the word "MENO"!

When Jesus instructs the believers to **ABIDE (the Koine' Greek word is MENO)** in him as a branch would abide in a vine, he is describing a **RELATIONSHIP that is defined by "PRESENCE"**. Here, two people (symbionts) undertake a **"SOJOURN" or JOURNEY together** in which they are continuously interacting with and mutually benefitting from each other --- providing something that EACH needs for its health and well-being. It may be unusual to think of God as "needing" something from us humans. However, God "needs" US in the sense that God's love MUST have expression. God made us out of love…and God loves us. **Love itself is ALWAYS directed TO another person or entity. Therefore, LOVE ALWAYS requires a recipient, a subject to RECEIVE it.** In this way, God's love "needs" us as the

AFFIRMATION #7:

recipients or subjects who can receive God love. In this sense, God "needs" us in order that God may express God's love and care. **And although we may NOT FULLY grasp or understand it, John is declaring that God mutually BENEFITS from the IN-DWELLING and INTERACTION with US as WE do in our interaction with God!!!**

In the Hebrew Bible or Old Testament, **the Prophet Jeremiah speaks in Chapter 17** to proclaim the same point that John later asserts in the New Testament. Jeremiah also writes the book of Lamentations in which he "laments" or "cries" or "wails" for the captivity of Judah and the destruction of the Temple in 587 b.c.e. What he also bemoans is that the reasons why such misfortune has befallen Judah is due to the community's own **DIS-connection** from the Divine Principles which Yahweh has handed down. Because of this **separation** or **disconnection**, Judah has acted in ways that are contrary to Divine Will. The **FRUITS** or actions and relationships which provide **EVIDENCE** of that **disconnection** can be seen, felt, and judged by Yahweh. The **FRUITS** which would indicate that Judah is practicing what is pleasing to God are nowhere to be found.

Jeremiah chooses the imagery of a TREE and its PRODUCE or FRUITS to represent Judah and its faithfulness to Yahweh. And so the words of the Prophet Jeremiah are delivered with unmistakable force and clarity. If Judah and its inhabitants place their **TRUST (FAITH, CONFIDENCE, LOYALTY)** in God, then they will be like..."a **TREE** planted by the waters...that spreads out her **ROOTS** by the river, and shall not see when heat comes, but her leaves shall be green,... and drought [shall not affect her]...neither shall [she] stop yielding her FRUIT."(vv.5-8).

Jeremiah identifies what a community **SUFFERS and LOSES** when it is **DIS-CONNECTED from the Source** of goodness, peace, justice, truth, and love. **Paul, writing to the Church at Galatia** delivers a message that **AFFIRMS** what John is advocating with his portrait of Jesus as the **TRUE VINE**. Paul tells the Galatian Christians what the community **GAINS** and how it is **BLESSED** when it is **CONNECTED to the Source** of goodness, peace, justice, truth, and love.

In Chapter 5, Paul offers a **glaring CONTRAST** between …. The **WORKS** (Greek = ERGA) of the FLESH (Greek = SARX) and the **FRUITS** (Greek = KARPOS) of the Spirit (Greek = PNEUMA). As I hear him, Paul is saying to us that whatever we think, say, and do that is **disconnected** from Divine Principles and based upon our own design, amounts to **OUR "WORK" (ERGON).** Such "work" is driven primarily by **our own EGO (Sarx)** and impulses which insist upon their own code of conduct – what we ourselves determine is right. For Paul this ego-driven "work" will lead inevitably to nothing good in the long run. WHY? Because these "works" are based upon something that is finite, limited, and conditioned by time, space, our own attachments to our culture, geography, education, upbringing, loyalty, training, desires, and beliefs.

John reminds us that what is LASTING is BEYOND OUR OWN "WORK". As the Apostle Paul would say, the Christian life, is based upon **something greater and more lasting than our own "work"**. It is based upon a power and Source beyond us – namely **God's Divine Principles mediated to us by the Holy Spirit.** When we **ATTACH OURSELVES** to these principles…when we **KEEP THE COMMANDMENTS ("keep" comes from the Greek word TEREO which means to attend to something very carefully or to be a good steward and give special care to something)**.. when we do **"SPIRIT WORK"** (rather than OUR WORK)… we are at the same time **ABIDING IN CHRIST, THE TRUE VINE.** This allows us to **RELATE** to others in new and different ways. Our lives begin to **YIELD or PRODUCE** a specific set of behaviors. These are the **FRUIT of the Spirit** --- love, joy, peace, self-control, gentleness, compassion, goodness, faith. These are what branches (believers) produce when we **ABIDE in Christ**. All of these character traits result from believers being.. attached to….present with…traveling companions with Christ.

BUT!! This is not even the END of it all!!! What becomes clear when we place Jeremiah, Paul, and John in conversation is the **REAL, GENUINE REASON** for the instruction of Jesus to ABIDE**… Here, in**

AFFIRMATION #7:

<u>**John Chapter 15, we are given the Word**</u>.... **It is a CONDITIONAL Word... IF..IF..IF we ABIDE CONTINUOUSLY** --- dwell with, sojourn with, interact with, be present with, become **SYMBIONTS with Christ...** When we surrender to Divine Principles mediated through the Holy Spirit, **we GAIN A LOT!!!** Yes.. we gain ALL THE GOOD THAT GOD HAS PREPARED FOR US!! Yes... We produce **good FRUIT. (John uses the SAME word here (KARPOS) that Paul uses in Galatians Chapter 5).** Yes... We acquire traits of character and habits of behaving that empower relationships in a positive way.

BUT! The **AIM of ABIDING in Christ gives us even MORE** than this. **What we gain is the JOY that is IN CHRIST. WE will have a JOY in us that is NEVER depleted.** The word that John uses for **Joy here, in the Koine' Greek is CHARA.** It means delight, gladness, to rejoice, ecstasy, or exhilaration. The Greek word that John uses to <u>describe</u> the way that the Holy Spirit wants to **"GIFT" us** with this kind of joy is **PLERO'-O. It means to be filled to the brim, totally fulfilled or COMPLETE! This is the PRIMARY reason for abiding in Christ. We do Spirit work in order to continuously replenish the JOY of Christ that dwells in us.**

With this JOY we will not experience a need to turn to anything else (people, material possessions, addictions, achievements, etc.) to fill any void or emptiness we may feel within us. **Instead, we will experience a "JOY" that is FULL and COMPLETE as we remain connected to the TREE, the True VINE – as we ABIDE in Christ.** In this way, **our lives will produce good fruit as we remain connected to Jesus the Christ - the Tree, the True Vine.**

AFFIRMATION #8:

Seeds We Sow Determine the Harvests We Experience
Matthew 13:31-32

Have you ever attended a sermon, lecture or class excited, hoping to experience the thrill of learning something new, and the instructor, lecturer or preacher was having a difficult time "capturing" the attention of the listeners? ... Where the content of the subject matter seemed to be very interesting, but the person's ability to communicate that content to the audience was lacking? ... Where the communicator seemed to have simply "lost" the listeners? I can recall several such experiences. Ok.. Confession time!.. To be honest, I can recall at least one or two times when I have felt like this WHILE I WAS IN THE PULPIT PREACHING!!

What I have noticed each time this has occurred is: the communicators who recognized what was happening and who were successful in regaining the attention of the listeners in the audience had one simple device in their knapsacks ------ **STORIES!!!!** In virtually every case I witnessed, the preacher or lecturer who looked over the glassy-eyed, fidgety, numb audience used **STORIES** to recapture the interest and attention of the gathering.

Stories work! There is something in the human psyche that

AFFIRMATION #8:

responds to a story… and each time a story is introduced, the ears of listeners perk up and people lean forward into the story. I believe it is because stories present the listener with the probability that she or he will find themselves somewhere inside the characters or incidents of that narrative. In this way, the profound, deeper truths about ourselves and the world will be made less abstract and more clear ----- through the story.

Jesus in the Synoptic Gospels **uses stories a LOT**. Jesus must have experienced, upon occasion, listeners who were distracted or anxious or worried or who simply couldn't follow his message. When we remember that <u>**over ¾ or 75%**</u> **of the people in Jesus' day were functionally illiterate, uneducated, poor SLAVES**, we can see why Jesus was forced to use stories as a teaching device. Jesus, though, went a little farther in his instructional techniques. In order to communicate abstract concepts like the Kingdom of God, Kingdom of Heaven, sin and evil, or salvation, **Jesus also used what we call <u>PARABLES</u>!!!**

William Barclay's fascinating book, **<u>The Parables Of Jesus</u>** provides a lot of information about the use of parables in Jewish culture. It is eye-opening! As a Jew, Jesus was already predisposed to use parables as part of the teaching tradition employed by his ancestors to open peoples' minds to some part of God's truth. The Hebrew Bible or Old Testament, in fact, uses parables as a teaching device. You can see this In **2 Samuel 12:1-7** when the Prophet Nathan is sent by God to deliver a message to King David after he had coveted Bathsheba, and had her husband Uriah killed. OR.... take the writing of the Prophet **Isaiah 5:1-7** where Isaiah uses the parable of a vineyard and its fruit to raise the issue of moral misconduct in the nation of Judah.

Jesus took a common form of Jewish teaching and gave it new meaning and beauty to make it even more effective for his time. The Hebrew mindset was very practical. So, rather than arguing for argument's sake like the Greeks, Jews were much more interested in reaching conclusions. Since humans, then and now, tend to think in pictures, abstract ideas often are harder for us to grasp. **Jesus used pictures called parables in order to give his message a better**

chance of being understood. So Jesus used earthly experiences to lead peoples' minds to heavenly things. This is why a parable is often referred to as an **"earthly story with a heavenly meaning"**. Using parables, Jesus taught people to see the operation of the supernatural in what was natural, regular, and normal.

What is often overlooked is that virtually every one of the parables Jesus used were **produced instantaneously -- in the spur of the moment.** Parables are stories that are birthed with some sort of conflict or dilemma as the backdrop. For this reason, the parables Jesus told were aimed at persuading the listeners to **make a moral judgement on some familiar moral issue.** When Jesus finishes telling the parable, there is an immediate sense evoked in the hearers that they will have to **make some kind of judgement or decision - -- FOR OR AGAINST some idea, some behavior.** Those who heard the parable knew at once which side of the issue they were on. This is why Jesus' parables often evoked such anger in some of those present.

I can see why **a PARABLE is much more than simply a nice, entertaining story.** A **PARABLE** contains the kernel of a story... yes... BUT! A **PARABLE** goes just a step farther to offer a **COMPARISON** within that story – **a comparison between an abstract idea and something in the human experience that resonates with the listeners.** A PARABLE uses a comparison that is sometimes called a **SIMILE.** A SIMILE compares two things which, on the surface, may appear to be totally UNLIKE, in order to explain a complex concept or a deep truth. We use similes all the time. Have you ever heard the simile**, "LOVE IS A MERRY-GO-ROUND, BUT A MERRY-GO-ROUND IS NOT LOVE"?** This is a simile. It compares two things – love and merry-go-rounds -- that are Unlike each other in order to explain what one of these things is like.

If you place the <u>simile</u> above in a **<u>parabolic form (parable)</u>**, it might sound something like this: **Love is like a woman who went to a carnival one day. She had been having a rough 3 weeks with her husband – arguments, fights, awkward silences, feelings of isolation and abandonment. While at the carnival, a man noticed her**

AFFIRMATION #8:

demeanor and began to talk with her. She told him her story… When she asked him what he thought she should do, he pulled 2 tickets out of his pocket. They were for 2 rides on the carousel. A little confused, she rode the carousel for a while… got off… and got right back on for her 2nd ride… She rode for over 40 minutes. When she got off. She said to herself, "you know what… I guess this is what experiencing a love relationship is like. It's like a merry-go-round. When you get on it, you already know that you ain't goin' nowhere… but… when you off of it, you sho' know you been someplace!" This is a **PARABLE!!** – a story that offers a simile (comparison) between two things --- love and riding a merry-go-round. Jesus used this teaching device on many occasions to get across deep spiritual ideas to his listeners.

When I consider what all of this means as I read **Jesus' PARABLE of the mustard seed in Matthew 13:31-32,** I am amazed at how such a small story can carry such enormous weight. **This parable is also a story used by the Gospel writers Mark and Luke.** As you might imagine, each writer uses this same parable to emphasize different aspects about the way spiritual faith and growth works. This Affirmation focuses on Matthew's aim. The clear point of the parable in Matthew is the fact that **OVER TIME, THE SMALLEST SEED GROWS INTO THE LARGEST OF TREES OR HERBS.** In Ancient Palestine, the mustard seed was commonly used to indicate the smallest of all things. Actually, **the CYPRESS SEED** was even smaller than the mustard seed. However, the cypress seed never gained the popularity of the mustard seed for expressing the smallness of something.

Mustard seeds are thick little black seeds that are so small they could fit on the head of a safety pin. And yet, Mustard trees commonly grew to heights of over 6 or 7 feet. And it is true that birds came and nested in its branches. **The parable spoke to several levels of meaning for Jesus. It had a special message for his disciples.** Jesus told it right when they were discouraged and fearful. At first, the crowds flocked out to hear Jesus. It looked like the promise of

John the Baptist that Jesus was the GREAT ONE whose movement would transform everything. It seemed that everything the movement was representing was going to come true. But then little by little the opposition to Jesus' message increased. The crowds slowly began to abandon him. Their hopes started to evaporate. Jesus told them this parable so they could hear that **they WERE THE SMALL SEED FROM WHICH THE MOVEMENT WOULD GROW.**

The parable also gives us a universal truth: **ALL THE GREATEST THINGS IN LIFE START FROM THE SMALLEST BEGINNINGS.** This growth most often happens beyond our ability to see it. The mustard seed is growing all the time. Over time -- not in a big flash -- gradually the seed's growth is in process. This is how progress is made! **Once planted, the seed becomes a WORK IN PROGRESS UNTIL FULL MATURITY IS ACHIEVED**. Finally, this parable speaks to **the process involved in PERSONAL CONVERSION EXPERIENCES.** Surrender to the Lordship of Jeshua ha' Meshiah is **an EVENT. A GIFT.** BUT! Along with this gift comes **a TASK**. Along with the event comes **a PROCESS.** The **TASK** is to gradually unwrap the gift of faith so that the fruits of the Holy Spirit can be displayed in our lives. **This involves a PROCESS called SANCTIFICATION**. Sanctification means **dying more and more each day to our OLD WAYS** of thinking and behaving (our EGO) … and **living more and more each day to GOD'S NEW WAYS** of thinking and behaving (the Holy Spirit). Jesus tells **the parable of the mustard SEED** to communicate all of this to his disciples and listeners.

And speaking of **SEEDS**….., growing up as I did on a farm, I came in contact with ALL types of seeds. My father would go to the local "feed and seed" store and buy seeds during planting time. He would come home with Kroger sacks filled and popping to the brim with peach, apple, mulberry, pear, corn, cotton, green peas, turnip green, and green bean seeds. With his mule and plow, and beat up old tractor, my brothers and I watched him plow up the ground, "rake" the big clods of dirt to make them smooth, and "drop" or

AFFIRMATION #8:

plant these seeds.

I wanted to grow things like my father. **So, I developed a fascination with seeds and plants.** I remember once when I had caught the planting "bug" as Southerners would call it, I went to the seed and feed store by myself to buy some seeds. For some unexplainable reason, along with okra, corn, cabbage, and tomato seeds, I proceeded to buy a small bag of orange seeds! I dug up a small patch of ground, "raked" it, and planted the seeds, and watered them religiously. To my delight, the seeds sprouted and grew into plants, and produced yield in various degrees. The okra plants grew so much until they took over the patch of ground. Tomatoes also came up, and I had enough to use on my salads and sandwiches. As for the corn, the stalks grew but were so hard and dry we could only manage to eat a few. **All the seeds produced EXCEPT --- the oranges!!** Not one of the orange seeds produced anything. I later found out that the climate in Mississippi was not good for orange trees. I now know that I would have been more successful growing oranges if I had been in Florida!! Oh well...... we live and learn!!!

Well into my eighties now, I have come a long way from planting seeds as a girl in Mississippi to becoming ordained as a minister of the Gospel. **What I can see much more clearly now is that planting seeds and being good stewards of their growth process is very much like preaching Good News to people whose souls are hungry, wounded, and anxious.** The Words of the Gospel are the "seeds". The preacher is the planter. The people are the "soil" or "ground" – the condition of the heart and soul. The seeds are always ready to be "dropped" or planted. **However, when the seeds are "dropped", their chances of producing is very much dependent upon the "climate" or consistency of the "soil" – the condition of the heart and soul.**

Sometimes, life experiences has caused the "soil" to be fallow, suspicious, and uncaring. At times, the "soil" is confused and lacking direction. At other times, the "soil" is hurt or wounded from traumas it has suffered. The soil is important, and so is the type of seed we plant. Seeds of anger, disrespect, and argument lead to "harvests" of divisiveness and mistrust. I have learned that… you can't plant okra seeds and expect to reap an onion harvest…. and… You cannot plant orange seeds in Mississippi and expect them to yield like they would in Florida or California. **I have learned and RE-learned that if I want to reap love, peace, trust, and joy, I have to "plant" or "drop" these SEEDS in the "soil" or "souls" of those with whom I am in relationship. I have learned and RE-learned that** the Seeds We Sow Determine the Harvests We Experience.

AFFIRMATION #9:

Tact, Self-Control & Humility are Marks of Spiritual ` Maturity

2 Corinthians 6; Galatians 5

"Don't mind her. You'll have to excuse her. She doesn't mean any harm. It's just the way she is. She's always been that way. We just have to get used to it. She's just being who she is..."

These are a few of the statements that I have heard people use to describe persons who are irascible, ill-tempered, and irritable in their dealings with others. These descriptions are dangerous, I believe, because they legitimate a way of relating to others that excuses personal accountability. They enable people to continue to behave towards others without any consideration of others' feelings. They allow people to run roughshod over others' worth and dignity without thinking about the consequences of their behavior. This, I believe, is morally wrong. There is no way that I can see where relating to others without counting the costs will result in a healthy relationship.

I believe that what we are talking about, in the final analysis, is **MATURITY.** Psycho-emotional maturity, spiritual maturity, relational maturity... **MATURITY!** When we excuse behavior that demeans others, devalues others, or fails to consider the humanity and dignity of others, then we are engaged in enabling persons to remain

IMMATURE relationally.

Maturity is a word that you probably have heard tossed around many times in many settings. I know I have. BUT! Have you ever been a part of a discussion that was focused on defining what maturity actually means? I believe we need to know precisely WHAT it means in order to counter immature ways of relating to others --- and ourselves.

MATURITY could be defined as…the state of being fully developed as a person at multiple levels of being. A person is thought to be "mature" at the point where she or he demonstrates the physical, mental, psychological, emotional, social qualities or skill sets of stable thinking and sound decision making. There are many **"signs"** of a person's "maturity", according to psychologists --- the capacity to recognize and verbalize when you are wrong or have made a mistake; an awareness of the biases that you harbor; the capacity to accept differences of opinions and lifestyles without being judgmental; the capacity to create a space between your feelings and your reactions (being able to have control over your emotions); taking responsibility for yourself and your decisions and actions; being able to accept yourself for who and what you are regardless of others' opinions about you; realizing and verbalizing how much you DON'T know; the capacity to exhibit compassion, humility, and a consideration of others' thoughts and feelings.

If you've ever heard the phrase, **"Act your age, and not your shoe size"**, you were hearing a call to maturity. If you've heard the phrase used often in the South, **"The trouble with some young people is they want to be grown up too fast… and the problem with some old folks is that they want to stay young too long"**…you were hearing a call to maturity.

Immature thoughts and behaviors are driven by a hidden form of self-seeking or self-enhancement. This is nothing more than **self-centeredness** – an overblown fixation on one's own needs and desires at the expense of others. The motivations of an immature personality are "mixed", and underneath is an aim of **self-seeking**. As a person matures, the thoughts and behaviors come to be driven less and less by a desire to **self-serve**, and more and more from a deeper level of

AFFIRMATION #9:

awareness within.

From a spiritual perspective, the Christian tradition refers to this maturity development as **the PROCESS of SANCTIFICATION**. Sanctification is a journey that is pushed along by **TWO (2) experiences that occur simultaneously.** These experiences are called mortification and vivification. As you can see, mortification has to do with death, and it is described as more and more each day **DYING** to everything in our lives that tends to separate or block our connection with God. Vivification has to do with life, and it is described as more and more each day **LIVING** or focusing upon everything that enhances or deepens our connection with God. Sanctification is a **PROCESS.** It represents **a "JOURNEY".** It doesn't complete itself instantly. Rather, it requires a continuous "walking and seeking" on a path that leads to a destination that none of us arrive at fully in this life. The process of sanctification is expressed clearly and beautifully by the **PRAYER** we highlighted in Affirmation #6:

Day by day Dear Lord, of Thee three things we pray; to SEE Thee more clearly; to LOVE Thee more dearly; and to FOLLOW Thee more nearly day by day!

Paul reminds the church at Corinth and us, that we are ALL WORKS IN PROGRESS! We are ALL flawed, imperfect human beings UNDER CONSTRUCTION! We are being made complete each day on the journey, as we focus on living a **more AUTHENTICALLY "Christian" life.** The influence of the presence of the Holy Spirit in our lives is transformative in its effect. This means that over time, as maturing humans, we are expected to see improvement in our lives in every sphere of activity – thoughts, words, and deeds. If we want to measure how our development as disciples of Christ is coming along, we have but to look at how we are demonstrating the **"MARKS" OF MATURITY.**

Paul's focus in 2nd Corinthians Chapter 6 is upon SPIRITUAL MATURATION. Paul speaks to the church at Corinth to promote the idea that the power of the Holy Spirit works on each person to counter the negative words and acts we use to relate with others. And in so doing, it undercuts any explanations or excuses we may want to make for our behaviors. In this way, **the Holy Spirit works at cross-purposes with our egos to "check" the immature thoughts and behaviors that we harbor and put forth.** The Holy Spirit is working to guide us on **a PATH to MATURITY.** There are, of course several "marks" of spiritual maturity. Paul, again, lifts these up in his description of **"FRUITS OF THE SPIRIT" in Galatians Chapter 5.** Notice, he contrasts these fruits or "marks" with human "works" which come from the EGO and which manifest in immature outcomes. I want to briefly **highlight THREE (3) of these "MARKS" or "SIGNS"** of a person who is following a path of spiritual maturity ---- **TACT, SELF-CONTROL, AND HUMILITY.**

Tact may be understood as the ability to deal with others without creating or enhancing offense. **Self-control** may be understood as resisting the urge to say or do something IN-appropriate in a situation. **Humility** may be understood as the capacity to subject oneself to Self-critique. Attention to just these 3 "marks" has an immediate, deep and positive impact upon the quality of our relationships with other humans. They are Spirit-driven rather than ego-driven. They are "signs" or "indicators" of a person's growth and development on the path of spiritual maturity.

I am thinking now of **a woman** who is just absolutely brilliant as a banking/financial investor and advisor. She can do with numbers what Jesus could do with parables. She has won many awards for her achievements in the banking world, and she has helped many, many people and their families move from major debt to a solid income stream. Without question, she is a giant in the world of finance. BUT!!! She is a dwarf in the world of healthy relationships. **She remains a spiritually and relationally immature woman.** She is messy in her dealings with others. She is choppy and short-tempered with people. She discounts others' opinions. She cusses folk out at the drop of a hat. She yells at her colleagues and treats them as if they are undeserving of basic respect and dignity. She is a "poster child" for what an EGO-driven, immature personality looks like when it relates to others. Her way of relating to

AFFIRMATION #9:

others is completely contrary to what scripture directs. **Spiritual maturity** demands tact and humility in our relating to others. **Spiritual maturity** demands a seeking, an intentional focus on achieving a more solid alignment of our emotions and our intellects. **Spiritual maturity** demands a "check" on what we say and do as we relate to others so that we will help and heal rather than divide and harm.

I can see the ways in which tact, self-control, and humility inevitably lead to relational outcomes that are positive rather than divisive. I married at a very young age of 16 years. Since my husband and I were not financially able at the time, we lived with his mother for a while. She was a Godsend to us! I learned a lot from her about housekeeping and homemaking. However!!!! She had a controlling, "bossy" personality, and virtually always insisted upon her own way in all matters. Her "advice" always came across as an "order" since she would push until we gave in, accepted her "advice", and did things her way.

When we moved into our own house, my mother-in-law continued to use coercive tactics to force us to do things her way. There was one particular habit that she performed regularly and religiously upon her visit. She would come into the house, rearrange the furniture as well as portraits hanging on the walls to HER satisfaction. I felt instinctively, at that time, that to challenge her and confront her behavior would lead to nothing but divisiveness. Since my husband would not confront his mother about the impropriety of her behavior and its negative consequences, I felt that I was left with no support. I knew she was "mouthy" and "pushy" and not prone to take criticism well. I knew that she would not simply do as I asked. She would not go away quietly and give in to my requests to stop. It would escalate the situation. So I smiled as I watched her come in, rearrange pictures and furniture, and instruct me as to what looked better when it was arranged HER way... And when she left, I would get up, rearrange the pictures and furniture right back in the way I had it before. When she would return, she would rearrange it all HER way, again! When she left, I would rearrange things MY way, again! We kept up this circular passive-aggressive pattern of relational behavior until she died. And we never had a cross word nor argument about any of it.

My husband's brother was also married, and my mother-in-law would ALSO behave in the very same way when she visited his home. In contrast though, my brother's wife behaved the very opposite way. Her approach was to challenge and confront my mother-in-law. She would verbally argue with her and tell her to leave her things alone because it was HER house HER things HER furniture and HER pictures. And she would do things HER way!! This NEVER ended in a positive fashion. We were always drained emotionally after these encounters. My mother-in-law was silent and brooding. My husband and his brother were silent and frustrated. My sister-in-law was seething and unsatisfied and in a negative emotional state. Nothing good happened. We couldn't have lunch or dinner afterwards as we had planned because the mood was so toxic. I am not claiming that MY way was the BEST way, BUT!!! I can see how, despite my mother-in-law's inappropriate behavior, my sister-in-law's approach left everyone in need of healing because it lacked tact, self-control, and humility.

Maturity takes note of the "big picture" of life and considers the consequences or possible impact of our behavior on others as well as our own lives. **Maturity** promotes empathic understanding of others. It tries to walk in the shoes of others and thinks about the well-being of others. **Tact** tries to work with others and love them even when they may be behaving in ways that are NOT loveable. **Humility** puts aside one's ego needs to be right or to have one's way in favor of assuming a peaceful, loving response that will help and heal a situation rather than elevate tensions and disagreements. **Humility** says, "I will take the high road of love and peace. I will subordinate my need to be right or to be in control. I will remind myself that I am ALSO an imperfect, flawed, conditioned person who just may be wrong in my thinking and assumptions. I will interrogate myself. I will perform my own self-assessment. And I will seek the path of love in this situation for a cause that is greater than myself." **Self-control** says "I will impose discipline and self-restraint so that I won't contribute to the madness but rather help to diffuse the tension and help to heal the situation." In my own

AFFIRMATION #9:

case, it was worth it to apply tact, self-control, and humility in dealing with my mother-in-law. By taking this approach, we remained very close until she died, even after her son and I had long been divorced. **Tact, Self-Control & Humility Are Marks of Spiritual Maturity.**

AFFIRMATION #10:

Elders of Excellence Are Wisdom Carriers

1 Peter 2:9; Acts 1:8

ELDERS.....OF....EXCELLENCE......ARE.....WISDOM..... CARRIERS....

When you slow this statement down, and say it while accentuating EACH word, you come to see that this is a mouthful to digest! What are **ELDERS?** What does it mean to claim something or someone is **EXCELLENT?** What is **WISDOM?** What does it mean to be a **CARRIER?**

An **ELDER** is thought of as <u>**a person of a greater age**</u> than most others. While human beings are living longer and experiencing more in their lives, <u>**persons who have reached the age of 65 or more**</u> are considered **Elders** in our Western culture. **Elders** also are associated with another element along with chronological age. **Elders** are <u>**valued for their wisdom and accumulated knowledge**</u> about life. EXCELLENCE may be understood as the quality of being <u>**considered outstanding or extremely accomplished or adept**</u> in some aspect. **WISDOM** involves the <u>**application of what a person knows or has learned**</u>. To be considered "wise", it is not enough for a person to merely "know" something. **Wisdom** is more than "knowing".

AFFIRMATION #10:

Wisdom is the **consistent, repeated application** of what a person knows. A **CARRIER** is a person or object that **holds and transmits** something. A **carrier transports and delivers** sought-after "goods". A **carrier bears and conveys or passes on** some information or item that is thought to be a valued "good" to others.

The Affirmation that **"Elders of Excellence are Wisdom Carriers"** involves a LOT! **It is a PACKED claim... and it is DYNAMIC!** When you step back and take a focused look at this statement while considering each aspect of its claim, you may experience an AHA!" moment similar to the one I had. While reflecting on this claim, I had an EPIPHANY about the BIG PICTURE "takeaway" from this statement which I could state below:

Human beings who have lived many years in terms of their age (ELDERS), more than likely have accumulated a lot of experiential knowledge. If these humans are able to pull life lessons from this considerable experience, they are more than likely to become "mind trusts" or "reservoirs of knowledge". They will CARRY tons of applied knowledge or WISDOM within. They will be stable thinkers. They will engage others with a balance of intellect and emotion. They will be persons whom the rest of us might want to "tap" or "pick their brains" in order to see what we might learn from them. In this way we would become more adept at navigating our own life paths – avoiding certain pitfalls and gravitating more towards what is good, easier, and productive. They will be able to assist us in our efforts to achieve EXCELLENCE in all that we might endeavor to achieve in our lives. These persons might serve as "life coaches" or "path clearers" who could save us lots of wasted time and energy when it comes to finding purpose, resolving conflicts, solving problems, managing relationships, achieving goals, experiencing joy, acquiring happiness, and making peace with our imperfections and mistakes in life.

I am led to believe that all of this points to **the ACQUIRING OF VIRTUES!!! Elders of excellence** are those persons who have managed to consolidate their total life lessons and experiences into a behavioral expression of **VIRTUES**. **Virtues and what it means to live a virtuous life** is something that is addressed in the sacred, authoritative texts of <u>**ALL**</u> the world's religions, including the Bible and Christianity. This topic is examined in <u>ALL</u> spiritual paths as well as the writings of philosophers and ethicists. This speaks to the importance that is placed on **virtuous living** throughout the centuries. So, it would behoove us, I believe, to at least examine what is meant by <u>**virtues and virtuous living**</u>, given its centrality in <u>ALL</u> sacred writings and all religious and spiritual traditions.

The definition of a **virtue** is multi-varied. There have been numerous understandings of **virtue** put forth over the centuries by many, many thinkers and writers. Upon reading these varied definitions, the notion of **VIRTUE** is not as simple as it might seem at first glance. However, as I see it, a **VIRTUE** may be defined as the **disposition and/or behavior which demonstrates high moral standards.** We could think of **virtue** as behavior which demonstrates moral excellence. It ALSO may be thought of as a **foundational principle or a trait or quality of one's character** which promotes doing what is right and proper and avoiding what is wrong or improper. Religious and spiritual traditions, philosophy, ethics, and each's authoritative writings identify specific dispositions and behaviors that are considered **VIRTUES**. These include courage, kindness, justice, temperance, prudence, patience, compassion, civility, honesty, faith, hope, love, fairness, tolerance, and **wisdom**, to name a few. So, when you boil it all down, a **VIRTUE** may be understood as **an INGRAINED DISPOSITION TO ACT OR BEHAVE IN ACCORDANCE WITH STANDARDS OF EXCELLENCE.** The focus on **VIRTUE**, which is found in <u>**ALL**</u> sacred writings throughout the ages, then, amounts to **a focus on CHARACTER. Character** is the key here, and the emphasis is upon forming the **virtuous character** in order to live a life of high moral quality.

There is one other element associated with **virtue** in ALL the sacred writings throughout the ages. <u>**ALL**</u> of these writings promote the idea that the **formation of virtue in one's character and living a life**

AFFIRMATION #10:

of high moral excellence must be acquired through <u>**REPEATED PRACTICE OVER TIME!!!!**</u> Becoming a virtuous human being, then, is **NOT** simply a decision or an affirmation or announcement. Virtuous living **DOES** involve CHOICE! And it **DOES** involve continuously AFFIRMING one's commitment to virtue on a daily basis! However, a virtuous character is acquired only through repeated practice over time.

What I can see now is that the accumulation of years may add up to an aged person. BUT! Being an aged person does <u>NOT</u> add up to a virtuous life. While I believe that ALL older persons deserve to be valued and respected for the years they have lived, I see clearly now that not all older persons are able to live **VIRTUOUS lives** that will serve as **a MODEL of moral excellence** for others. Therefore, despite their many years of planetary living they are not able to be **MENTORS** who can help to **MOTIVATE** other younger human beings to live virtuous lives. What a shame! How sad! .....

Of course, being **a "Wisdom Carrier"** is only <u>ONE</u> of the <u>many</u> virtues that elders of excellence have developed as a practice. We could name a few more such as fairness, empathy, and compassion. **I just want to focus on this <u>one</u> aspect of virtuous living --- being a carrier and practitioner of wisdom"** --- in this Affirmation. Why? Because it seems to me that wisdom, along with love, is one of the things **MOST NEEDED and MOST MISSING** from our private relationships and our public conversations.

WISDOM is also one of the most-often quoted and yet most partially-understood **VIRTUES** in our culture. At times, we tend to think of wisdom as "being smart" or "intellectually gifted". We also tend to associate advanced age with wisdom. Neither of these understandings necessarily get to the heart of what it means to be a WISE person or a human being who practices the virtue of wisdom. **What is wisdom, then? What does it mean to be wise? What IS a wisdom-carrier?** Ancient Greek culture and the Christian Biblical text offer us some assistance in arriving at answers to these questions.

As I shared earlier in this Affirmation, I believe that **wisdom** involves the repeated, consistent application of what a person has learned over time or knows. **Wisdom** in the Christian tradition has been heavily influenced by the culture of what scholars call the Greco-Roman world. This culture was based upon concepts from Greek thought. **Wisdom** was one of the central concepts of this culture. **Wisdom** was the subject of many Greek playwrights like Aristophanes and Greek philosophers like Plato and Aristotle. **Wisdom** was virtually always cast in the feminine gender as a Goddess or woman. This is a point that is often overlooked but should be given serious examination! All of this becomes important when Christianity began to develop and spread throughout the Greco-Roman world through the missionary efforts of the disciples and especially Paul of Tarsus.

Wisdom, as a key concept in the culture, was also introduced in the texts of the Gospel writers of the New Testament who used Greek concepts to explain their ideas. Since the New Testament itself was written in Koine' Greek, many ideas and concepts of Greek thought, including **"wisdom"**, would find themselves embedded in all the New Testament writings. **In Greek language, wisdom is identified by the word SOPHIA, a woman!** Sophia may be understood as the capacity to be intelligent, skillful, smart, wise, and clever. It also means "learned" and "stable" in one's thinking and acting. It is applied to **a person who acquires knowledge and has the capacity to make good use of it.** In today's cultures, **Sophia** continues to be a popular, celebrated name given primarily to girls (**Sophus** for boys) to designate elegance, sophistication and inner beauty.

BUT! **Wisdom** is a very important concept in the entire Bible. The Bible, in fact, contains 222 verses that focus solely on **wisdom**. **Wisdom** is also heavily emphasized in the Hebrew Bible or Old Testament. The Old Testament devotes three (3) of its 39 books to what is referred to as **KETUV'IM or WISDOM WRITINGS** in the Hebrew language – Proverbs, Job, and Ecclesiastes. These writings are devoted exclusively to revealing the collective wisdom of generations of spiritually aware personalities. These writings make clear just how central and indispensable WISDOM is for successful human

AFFIRMATION #10:

living. **In Hebrew language, wisdom is identified by the word CHOKHMAH. Chokhmah** may be understood as a **capacity to discern or intuit what is happening as well as what is being called for, in a given situation. Chokhmah** is believed to be a GIFT that comes from Divine Wisdom or God's UN-limited ability to "be", "know", and "do". **Chokhmah in Hebrew and Sophia in Greek** BOTH appear throughout the Bible to designate persons, communities, and nations that are considered to be WISE.

Wisdom, or the lack of it, has been a prominent issue in my own life at certain points. At times when I wasn't even aware of it, **wisdom** was THE main element that was absent in my personal trials OR present in the resolution of my personal problems. I can recall an experience that happened early in my marriage. Again, I married at the very young age of 16. Admittedly, I was not as **"wise"** in some areas of my life as I needed to be… I was just too young in age. My husband and I agreed to divide and share the expenses of our new home. My husband was to be responsible for paying the mortgage and utilities. I was responsible for paying for groceries and taking care of the needs of our children. For a time, this agreement worked well. Everything was going along happily until one day I flipped the light switch in the kitchen, and nothing happened. There were no lights. ALL the lights were out! Within a few hours, I received a notice in the mail which informed me that the mortgage ALSO had NOT been paid in 3 months! As you may imagine, this was a cause of great distress for me. I wrung my hands, not knowing what to do or how to proceed.

At the time, I had an older friend in my life whom I called immediately. After listening to my frantic speech for a while, she finally said, **"Listen, baby… you work. Don't' you?! You work, so you pay your own mortgage and your own utility bills. Pay them first before you buy any food or clothes or anything else. You go down to those companies and make an arrangement TODAY to pay these bills. You take care of yourself and make sure you keep a roof over your and your children's heads above everything else. Then** make sure y'all have food to eat. Everything else comes AFTER that!". My friend's **wisdom** came to me like a bolt of lightning into my brain. It awakened me to my own power to act on my behalf. I NEVER forgot that wise lesson that she gave me.

Later in my life I would be introduced to the **Serenity Prayer**. It says: **God Grant me the serenity to accept the things I cannot change... the courage to change the things I can... and the <u>WISDOM</u> to know the difference.** There's that word again! **WISDOM! Wisdom** as a **VIRTUE** which aims at excellence, is a quality of character that develops over time. **Wisdom** has to be practiced repeatedly in order to become a more permanent component of a person's identity and way of living. As I got older, I would come to learn what **wisdom** really means and how valuable it is as a trait or virtue in one's character. I would come to understand **wisdom** as the capacity to repeatedly practice love, unbiased or balanced judgement, compassion, self-critique, the seeking of self-knowledge, benevolence, the desire to pursue sound decision making, and a desire to "see" the total or big picture in every experience. As I now enjoy life at the age of 83, I am praying for more **wisdom** as a virtuous practice in my character. I understand at a much deeper level that **Elders of Excellence Are Wisdom Carriers.**

AFFIRMATION #11:

The Good News Calls Each of Us to Moral Agency
Mark 1:14-15

For a long time, when I would reflect upon **examples of moral agency connected to the lives of black women**, I encountered a "block". My "block"? I thought immediately about Rosa Parks. She is certainly deserving of being identified as a **moral agent**, and she is also a black woman. What caused my "block"? I could not think about local, grassroots black women who lived everyday underneath the radar of the public news as **moral agents**. I never thought that there were black women whom I knew and who attended the same church with me, who should be considered **"moral agents"**. I believe this was because at that time I didn't really know **how moral agency and black women's experiences were connected with Jesus' Good News Gospel**.

As I began to learn more about **moral agency**, I came to see that I DID know a black woman who had demonstrated moral agency as a result of her commitment to Jesus' Good News Gospel. That woman was my own daughter. In the Spring of 1983, our church was beginning its "transition" from a middle-aged membership to a **"young adult" membership**. Our church's average age dropped sharply from 56 years to 37 years. This was fueled by a rapid influx of these young adults whose average age was 24 years. They were more educated, had higher paying jobs, traveled and read more extensively. They also were more abreast of current social and political news and they wanted the church to become more **relevant** to the issues of the time. **The young adults were asking what Jesus' Good News Gospel had to say about violence, democracy, voting rights, racism, poverty, crime, war, and – SEXISM. Yes ---- SEXISM!**

My daughter was one of these "young adult" members. As a young, married mother and black woman, she had helped lobby for a class that dealt with religion and contemporary issues. She also began to challenge the church about its sexist practices. One night at our weekly bible study, she stood and asked the men why women in the church were NOT allowed to hold the office of Deacon. She wanted to know where in the gospel did it explicitly deny women this right. She told the church that women made up 75% of the membership but represented only 2% of its decision-making office holders.

A heated debate followed. ALL the men present were clearly AGAINST women becoming Deacons, and so were a few of the women. They used Paul's injunctions in **I Corinthians 14:34 and I Timothy 2:11-12** to argue on scriptural grounds that women should NOT hold office over men. My daughter was versed in this area and countered with a history of women's roles in the early church. She also lifted up the role of black women during slavery and Jim Crow segregation and the civil rights movement. I don't remember much of the dialogue from that meeting, but I DO remember a few points she made that shut the debate down. She said that racism was morally wrong and that no scripture could ever make HER agree that it was right. She said that white people used the Bible AGAINST black people to argue that we were slaves. She said black men did NOT accept this, so why should women accept arguments that women should be subordinate to men in the church. Then she said, "what do I tell my daughter who is only 2 years old?... that because she is a woman, she can NEVER hold ANY office in THIS church, even though she may be better equipped, qualified and dedicated than any

AFFIRMATION #11:

man in this church?" She said that sexism was morally wrong too, and no scripture could ever make her agree with it or accept that it was morally right. Then she sat down!!! The silence was deafening!!!

The pastor asked us all to stand and stated that the devil was trying to break up the church and that we shouldn't allow him to do it. Then he sang a doxology and dismissed us. Leaving aside my own biased feelings for a minute, I remember that this event which occurred on a Wednesday night had filtered throughout the church by Sunday morning... and it was a cause of division. Most people thought my daughter was stirring up trouble. They felt she should be supportive of black men since they were so maligned and discriminated against in the culture. Others felt that the scriptures were clear that God wanted men in charge, NOT women.

My daughter and her husband left the church in a few months to live in another city and state. BUT! The "shakeup" they left was there to stay and would NOT go away. Other young women in the church began to raise similar questions about the church's sexist practices. Eventually most of these young women left the church. They did NOT feel that our church was a loving, caring, supportive, and empowering community for women.

I was NOT pleased that so much negative talk and feelings were the result of something that my own daughter had started. Now, I know that she was merely demonstrating **moral agency**, and she was practicing this as a result of her commitment to the Good News Gospel of Jesus Christ. To her, this gospel was mandating that <u>ALL</u> forms of subordination, discrimination, and devaluation, be unmasked, challenged, and defeated. To her, sexism was morally wrong because it violated the values of love, justice, and inclusiveness that the Gospel had proclaimed as central to the church's true identity. I would come to believe, as I do now, that she was on to something. She was right! My daughter, in her own way, was practicing **agency**.

What does it mean to claim that Jesus' Good News Gospel amounts to a call to moral agency? What had my daughter picked up on that so many in our church had overlooked or completely missed? I believe that we have to first ask ourselves, "What IS agency?" **AGENCY may be understood as action designed to produce a particular effect such as an intervention of some kind.** Agency is based on a belief in the capacity of persons to act independently and make free choices. **Agency** believes that humans can analyze situations, deliberate, make decisions, and act upon these decisions. **Agency** assumes that in any situation, there are options available to a person or group, and that these options can be identified, chosen, and acted upon with the aim of producing a desired outcome.

Agency, then, is about one's power to act! Action assumes that **POWER** is involved in every exchange between individual humans and groups. While power may be UN-equally distributed in a particular situation, **agency assumes that power is MULTI-VALENT. That is, power is NEVER the sole possession of one person or group.** **Agency** assumes that there are NO powerless persons or groups. There are ALWAYS **residuals of power** lying around to be used, even by people who have LESS **power** than others. **Agency** believes that there is ALWAYS enough **power** available to be used, even by those who are victimized or marginalized in any situation --- the power to resist, the power to confront and challenge, the power to name and explain, the power to advocate for love, justice, and truth, the power to motivate and change, and yes…even the power to forgive and heal.

Moral Agency sharpens this discussion. **MORAL AGENCY emphasizes an individual's ability to make moral judgements based on a notion of right and wrong, AND to take actions based on that judgement.** In this way, **MORALS** (standards for determining what behavior is right or wrong) are important in discussing **moral agency**. **Moral agency** ALSO entails a person's willingness to be held accountable for the judgements they make and the actions they take. **Moral agency** brings **moral values** into the forefront of the discussion. A **Moral Value** can be understood as a reality which guides, orients, and motivates humans thinking and behavior in light of a particular set of standards about what is right and wrong. **Moral**

AFFIRMATION #11:

agency, then, invites actions on the basis of some standard of right and wrong while assuming accountability for those actions.

As I reflect upon my daughter's actions during the time of her challenge to the church's sexist practices in the early 1980's, I can now identify her as a **moral agent**. She assumed the power to confront what she thought was wrong, unjust, and immoral. Her actions were based upon a standard (moral values) which she had taken from her understanding of **Jesus' Good News Gospel**, which she had been taught by the same church whose policies and practices she was now challenging. Is this what the Good News does to people, I thought? Does it make them restless and dissatisfied with what was once tolerable? **What is the Good News** and what about it fueled my daughter's and other women's discontent?

The Greek word is **"EUANGELION"**. It translates as **"Gospel" or "Good News"**! This word is used to describe the **CONTENT** of the message of Jesus and his disciples in the narratives of the New Testament. The Good News Gospel's **MESSAGE** is about Jesus' coming as the Messiah, announcing the coming of the Kingdom of God, and the offering of salvation to all humankind. The Gospel of **Mark 1:14-15** is a prime example of what Jesus' GOOD NEWS Gospel is about. Jesus begins his ministry to the world as a 3-fold effort of **preaching, teaching, and healing**. His efforts announce his intentions to challenge, confront, and "plunder" the negative, inhumane effects of the Kingdom of Satan (the Evil One).

For the culture of the times, the Good News Gospel comes as **an oppositional reality** to the prevailing culture of the day. The good news is that God has now provided **NEW POSSIBILITIES** for a NEW way of being --- a NEW way of seeing and understanding things, a NEW series of questions to be asked, a NEW cluster of responses to be made, a NEW way of conceiving how to live a more humane life under IN-humane conditions.

What is <u>ALSO</u> a key component of Jesus' Good News Gospel is its **invitation for decision and action**. There is a NEW day, and persons now have to choose between the old ways of living and the new possibilities it offers. This amounts to **a "CALL"! The Good News Gospel announces new possibilities while at the same time issues a moral imperative to ACT!** A **CALL** to repent, believe, and live one's life in accordance with a new set of moral values. Mark's Gospel is focused on this aspect of Jesus' ministry. **Mark is intent upon capturing the PROACTIVE element.** He uses the Greek word **"EUTHUS"** which translates as **"STRAIGHTWAY" or "IMMEDIATELY"** some **41 times** throughout the entire book to describe the focused, intense, energy Jesus uses as he does his "work" in the culture. Jesus performs **over 38 MIRACLES** in Mark, demonstrating his **POWER** to heal, save, and transform reality. Jesus is all about immediate action! His Good News is about **new possibilities AND new MANDATES for thinking and behaving.**

As we have already noted, this is about **AGENCY!** The **active engagement** of Jesus' preaching, teaching, and healing amounts to **the practice of moral agency.** Jesus **INVITES** individuals to **ENTER** into this **NEW** Kingdom as a disciple (learner and practitioner) of this **NEW** 'WAY". This is the CALL! The **"CALL"** of Jesus' Good News Gospel amounts to **a CALL to engage life as a moral agent.**

All of this places an inescapable demand upon those of us who choose to accept Jesus' invitation. **To answer "YES!" to the CALL of Jesus' Good News Gospel, then, is to make a decision to live as a moral agent.** There is NO way around it. Without question, **the NEW Vision of Jesus CALLS us to moral agency.** It invites us to think, speak, and act using moral values of love, justice, and peace as our standards of right and wrong while assuming accountability for our thoughts, words, and deeds. When we are genuinely awakened and committed to the values and vision of Jesus' Good News Gospel, we cannot ever fully go back to sleep. We certainly may nod off every once in a while, but we will not ever be in a deep sleep again.

There are many thoughts, words, and behaviors in our culture that are an OFFENSE to the Good News Gospel of Jesus Christ. We all can see these "offenses" in terms of relationship violence, discriminatory conduct, and policies that subordinate and demean others. We

AFFIRMATION #11:

all can observe these "offenses" in all areas of our society including our religious communities. **The seeker/disciple has made a choice for a NEW vision.** This decision means that the seeker/disciple has now taken upon her/himself the mandatory "yoke" of **moral agency** in light of a particular set of **moral values**. There is simply NO way to escape it.

This was the decision that my daughter made in the early 1980s when she confronted sexist beliefs and practices in our church. She made a choice for **moral agency**, and with that choice she made a decision to become marginal in our community of faith. I wonder now how it was that so many of us could <u>NOT</u> see **the CALL to moral agency** that was deeply embedded in Jesus' Good News Gospel. Maybe we were just too captive to the "traditional" ways of thinking and behaving. Perhaps we were too afraid of change and the uncertainty that it would unleash.

I know now that the CROSS which is the symbol of Jesus' Good News Gospel has TWO (2) Beams --- one Vertical and one Horizontal. I now know that the vertical beam represents our connection to God while the horizontal beam represents our connection to each other as humans. I now know that BOTH beams are important!!! BOTH beams place a moral imperative – **a CALL** – upon the life of the seeker/disciple. I now know that one beam cannot be sacrificed at the expense of the other. The vertical beam is very important. We ought to work on our relationship with the Divine. BUT! So is the horizontal beam. We MUST ALSO engage in the **moral agency** that is called forth by the horizontal beam.

When we commit to Jesus' Good News Gospel, we can expect a **TRANSFORMATION of consciousness in light of Jesus' Vision of a NEW way of thinking, acting, and BEING.** We can expect a moral imperative or **CALL for moral agency**... to now work towards OUTER manifestations of the new INNER world within us. We can expect to be **CALLED** to "engage" or participate in the "political". By "political", I do NOT refer to electoral politics, but rather 'politics' with a "little p", which should be understood as **"how we organize** our collective lives together". In this way, **the "personal"** (the call of the vertical beam to be concerned about my own connection to Divine Principles) now immediately **becomes inseparable** from **the "political"** (the call of the horizontal beam to be concerned about my relational connection to others) in Jesus' Good News Gospel. This is why sexist practices (part of the "political") HAD to be challenged as morally improper in the church's congregational life.

I believe that **moral agency** is ALSO about **INITIATIVE. Initiative means seeing what is REQUIRED… what HAS to be done in the situation, and DOING it!** It is about being a SELF starter, and it is a key element of **agency**. I am aware that some of us are slow starters. In situations which are calling us to some type of **agency**, many of us appear to be much slower than some others of us. Some of us are just plain hesitant, and even flat out resistant to assuming **personal moral agency** in this regard.

Thank God that there are others of us who hear **the call to agency** and act decisively for the greatest good in the situation at hand. I give thanks for organizations like **Black Lives Matter, White People for Black Lives Matter, Green Peace, MADD, Domestic Violence Hotline, Rape Crisis Center, Citizens Against Food Desserts, Community Job Retraining Programs, and others** who are demonstrating **agency** in our culture. I am grateful for those human beings who hear **the call to moral agency** in their lives and courageously act, dedicate their lives in causes much greater than themselves. These persons are involved in a wide range of actions designed to elevate the quality of life for millions of others --- working to achieve peace initiatives and promoting conflict resolution strategies; addressing domestic violence and unjust policing practices; focusing on voting equity, health care accessibility and eliminating poverty in our midst; working towards inclusivity and sustainable community development; advocating for the elimination of sexist policies and practices; AND working for justice, love, and peace in our religious communities (seeking to level the playing field for women seeking ordination in light of the mandate of Galatians 3, for example).

AFFIRMATION #11:

All of these examples represent persons and groups who have heard the call to moral agency. The Good News also calls each of us, as people of the "Way" (Christians) to moral agency. I pray that we hear and respond, with initiative, to this important Divine beckoning.

AFFIRMATION #12:

Everyone Needs Guidance from Time to Time as We Travel the Road Of Life
Isaiah 30:21; 42:16

It is perhaps one of the most well-performed comedic caricatures in the history of the modern stage. What is it? It's the humorous probe into the stubbornness and egocentricity of the male mind. It's such an interesting and compelling "mystery" that **PsychCentral Magazine** published an entire article dealing with this subject a few years back in 2014. The article was written by a PhD in psychology, Linda Sapadin. The title? **"Why Men Don't Ask for Directions".** Sapadin, chose a very interesting "hook" to cause the reader to lean into the story as an important matter. She opens, "Women often find the male mind hard to understand. Why can't men ask for directions when they are lost? Why can't they read an instructional manual when they don't know how to do something? Why can't they pore over a self-help book on relationships when it can help them enhance their [relationship] skills….An old adage is that women are emotional and men are logical…. So how come men don't operate rationally when they don't' know something?"

Sapadin explores this curious male approach to living and comes

AFFIRMATION #12:

away with **three (3) main cues** to help the reader understand why men behave as they do: **First,** Men prefer to learn by doing, not by being told what to do. **Second,** men want to win or emerge victorious on their own terms regardless of how long it takes or how difficult the task may be. **Third,** Men want to be strong. They don't want to be told what to do. Men would rather "suck it up" and do it "their way", even if "their way" makes the task more difficult.

What Sapadin has uncovered, I believe, has useful and instructive insights about men. However, I am becoming more aware that her insights are equally as true of women in our culture as well. The tendency to "go it alone" or act as a "rogue lone ranger" in life transcends gender. **BOTH men AND women appear to be equally "bitten" with the same "EGO bug"** that causes us to operate under the illusion that we are completely self-contained and self-sufficient...that we are capable of living a solitary life successfully, apart from any necessity to interact with or rely upon others....as if we could develop ourselves BY ourselves with-OUT any "guidance" or "assistance" from ANY other person. **This is the illusion of the myth of self-reliance** that has increasingly embedded itself into our **culture of narcissism, self-centeredness, and egomania...** and the effects of this illusion can be seen in virtually every area --- relationships, politics, education, religion, family, economics, (and especially!) social media!

As I was playing with my 3-year-old great grand-twins one afternoon, I was reminded of just how reliant they were upon their family to learn basic skill sets like walking, talking, reading, eating, and playing. When they were born, they didn't know anything about how to do these things. They were "guided" by the family – other human beings who loved them and cared for their wellbeing enough to take the time to assist them in their growth and development. As I write this affirmation, I am reflecting seriously on **what would be the outcome if my great grandtwins FORGOT about this GIFT of available and accessible GUIDANCE.** What if they, at some point in their lives, just stopped seeking it or welcoming it. How would they turn out?

NO ONE GETS TO BE WHO WE ARE ALL BY OURSELVES.

EVERY HUMAN BEING HAS REQUIRED GUIDANCE AND ASSISTANCE IN ORDER TO NAVIGATE THE PATH TOWARD MATURITY! EVEN IN OUR ADULT YEARS, WE STILL FIND OURSELVES IN SITUATIONS, AT TIMES, WHERE WE NEED THE GUIDANCE OF OTHER CARING PERSONS TO HELP US SOLVE PROBLEMS OR RESOLVE CONFLICTS THAT WERE TOO MUCH FOR US TO BEAR ALONE.

We ALL appear to recognize these truths at some deeper level of our consciousness. So why is it becoming so difficult for too many of us to ask for help or seek guidance and assistance when we're "stuck" or lost or confused? Who doesn't ask for directions when they're lost? Who doesn't get lost or misdirected or "off the beam" at times? **Who doesn't require "GUIDANCE" at times when we may be MIS-GUIDED or MIS-DIRECTED?**

The weight of these questions became real to me a few years ago **in 2008 during the shattering of the so-called "national housing bubble".** I can openly confess that this experience represents one of those times in my own life where **God's GUIDANCE** was offered to me, but I did NOT choose to hear it nor heed its direction. In the late 1990s, I had to serve as caregiver for my father and my aunt, both well into their 80s. I had re-married by then, and my second husband and I were still unsettled in our relationship. My children were all grown and gone now except my youngest adopted son. We lived in a small, cramped three-bedroom home, and we needed more space. So, I prayed about the matter and was led to a Christian real estate agent.

At this point, other Elders of the family advised against me buying a home. Based upon my age (70+ years) and our joint income streams (mostly Social Security Income plus my day work), the Elders of the family felt this was not sustainable for a monthly mortgage. They also felt it was too risky since my father's and aunt's incomes would be eliminated once they passed away. At their advanced ages, this was important to consider, but I didn't think too much about it. The Elders felt my decision was UN-wise and gave me sound reasons for their viewpoints, but **I decided that I would <u>NOT</u> hear nor heed their**

AFFIRMATION #12:

GUIDANCE. I didn't listen and decided that I would "trust in the Lord", as if this meant NOT listening to the Elders' wisdom.

I proceeded head-long into pursuit of a new home. I found one that I thought was perfect for us to all live in comfortably. In hindsight, I should have stopped when my husband, even prior to the Elders' admonitions, said that he would NOT go along with me in this venture. He said he did NOT want to, nor would he leave the home where we lived. This should have been enough to make me stop, slow down, and have some deeper conversations with him about why he felt as he did. BUT! It did NOT. Like a single woman, lone ranger, and community of one, I made all the calls, visits, had all the conversations, signed all the paperwork, made all the decisions – ALONE! I simply felt I knew best, and that I alone was right – even if no one else could see this. It was ME and JESUS, and that was enough for me. It never occurred to me at that time that Jesus was sending people in my life to help **GUIDE ME** to a better decision making and problem-solving process.

I had yet another experience of **Divine GUIDANCE** offered to me through a "warning" that should have been clear and instructive. I paid $20,000.00 down payment and the mortgage company then asked me to go back to my husband and talk to him about an important matter --- to THEM! They wanted me to convince him to sign a document that prevented him from suing THEM for any reason, even if the mortgage company put me out of the house for nonpayment. Again, that **inner voice of Divine GUIDANCE** spoke to me at that table, but again I disregarded it. I did NOT take heed.

We moved into the house and lived happily for about nine (9) years ---- UNTIL! BOTH my father AND aunt passed away within a year of each other. After their deaths, I received another slice of **God's GUIDANCE** in the form of yet another "warning" from a prophetess and several real estate agents that something turbulent was coming to disrupt the housing market. This was 2008, and every mortgagee like ME who did NOT have a fixed mortgage was going to be in danger of higher and higher applied interest rates. This meant that we (and our families) would lose our homes if we couldn't make the higher mortgage payments. None of us could since, like me, most of us were living off fixed incomes.

As you may recall, this period in our nation from 2008 until around 2012 was disastrous for about 7 million homeowners like me who were deemed to be living in "upside down" mortgages. This meant that our homes were now worth LESS than what we were paying for them in mortgage payments. All told, the housing experts say that for each owner like me who were affected, we should factor in 6 other persons who were also living in these homes along with the owners. This meant that over 42 million Americans were affected. In the end, 42 million Americans lost our homes. We were forced to move out, sell or put our homes up for public auction.

Later, my daughter went with me to companies like NACA to help me work out keeping the home, but to no avail. Even as we were working to help me, I knew I did NOT have the income NOR the energy to keep this home. Yet I would NOT accept nor heed the Divine GUIDANCE that was coming in the forms of my daughter and the NACA agents. I realize that this is a rather long accounting of an experience in my life, and to be brutally honest, I would rather NOT EVER share this experience --- NOT EVER!!! I include it in this Affirmation #12 because I believe it is instructive and offers to the reader some **valuable GUIDANCE** about **how important it is to openly seek out, listen to and heed GUIDANCE --- regardless of the form in which it appears.** To do so will save us valuable time, talent, treasure, heartache and heartbreak. This was a hard lesson to experience!

The popular stories of **the Wiz and the Wizard of Oz** capture the truth about **the absolute necessity for GUIDANCE in EVERY person's life.** These stories capture in a visually stunning and entertaining way, what happens when any of us settles down and gets intentional and focused about embarking upon an inner-directed journey. Dorothy and her friends are on a quest. This quest represents **the path that EACH of US must take to arrive at a deeper understanding of our TRUE Selves.** The quest amounts to a process, **a JOURNEY** which leads to a deeper knowledge of who we really ARE – our TRUE Selves.

AFFIRMATION #12:

Dorothy and her friends require lots and lots of help – **GUIDANCE!** – as they wind their way through the different surprise events, roadblocks, and pitfalls that they encounter along the way. They don't fully comprehend the signs and symbols. They don't really know what anything means because they are thrust suddenly into a totally new and different environment. **They ALL will need GUIDANCE!** And in the moments where they experience fear, stress, frustration and despair, there is always **some form of GUIDANCE** which makes itself available to them and enables them to get back on the path that will lead to the goal they are seeking.

In stories like these, we all tend to identify more with one of the characters. However, rather than seeing ourselves through a single character in the story, in actuality we are ALL of the characters in the narrative. **ALL of the characters are US! The characters represent different aspects of our total selves --- different states of our minds, different conditions of our hearts.** In the words of Jean Houston, the story could be called **The Wizard of US**! What is important to remember is that this **inward journey**, when taken seriously, **leads inevitably to a transformation of ourselves into the person we truly ARE – the person God intended US to become.**

BUT!!! Like the characters in this story, **not one of us can advance successfully on the path of inner transformation without GUIDANCE!** Guidance then functions to help keep us on the right path, and signals to us when we have taken detours or turned down dead end streets and blind alleyways. In our current culture, guidance functions like **the GPS Systems in our driving vehicles.** GPS systems are designed to calculate the best possible routes to your destination using your present location. These systems know more about what directions to take, and what lies ahead in terms of inaccessible roads, speed traps, and traffic accidents. When you **activate your GPS and REQUEST GUIDANCE**, the system calculates the best path for you to take. Then a voice sounds off, 'Please proceed to the highlighted route!". **It is now in the power of YOU, the driver, to heed the GUIDANCE** and direction of the GPS and when the driver **accepts** the **GUIDANCE** and proceeds as directed, good things happen.

This is a message that **the Prophet Isaiah** places into our ears with the volume set at "LOUD"! Isaiah's tenure as a prophet and royal advisor spans the administrations of 4 Kings. He has seen a lot and has amassed a huge pile of wisdom. In **Chapters 1--39**, Isaiah is concerned to afflict those who are comfortable in Israel, sounding exhortations and warnings to a nation that is **rapidly "losing its way"** and headed into captivity. Israel is in need of **GUIDANCE** to help the nation **"find its way"** back to God. In **Chapters 40--65,** Isaiah's aim is to comfort those who are afflicted. The key word in these chapters is "salvation". If the nation seeks **God's GUIDANCE**, hears and heeds to it, then the nation can expect to experience the promises of redemption.

What is rather surprising to discover is how Isaiah places the **petition for Divine GUIDANCE** in a central position in the nation's efforts to achieve redemption and release from captivity. Isaiah seems to be frantically pleading to Israel to ask God for wise counsel to access the ways of truth; for the ability to hear **GOD'S** Divine "voice" while making decisions; for Divine illumination in the midst of uncertainty. All these emphases in Isaiah, no doubt, have been recaptured as Isaiah read and re-read **the wisdom literature of the Psalmist** whose verses contain numerous references to **Divine GUIDANCE**.

When Isaiah sits down to write **Chapter 30, verse 21 and Chapter 42, verse 16,** his objective is to comfort Israel with the reality that **God is waiting to provide GUIDANCE and direction. All that is required is Israel's willingness to ask and remain open to receive it.** If you do this, Isaiah tells the nation, your ears will, **"…hear my words telling you THIS is the way, walk THIS path, and turn in the direction, right OR left, as I GUIDE you….it doesn't matter if you are suffering from spiritual blindness, I will still GUIDE you in paths you cannot see and have not known…although you will be in darkness, I will make the light shine before you, and I will make your crooked paths straight…I will GUIDE you! I will do all of this for you and never forsake you as long as you seek my GUIDANCE."** The Divine promises that Isaiah announces to the nation of Israel more

AFFIRMATION #12:

than 600 years before the birth of Jesus, are equally valid and available to those of us who are willing to believe, receive, and embrace them in 2021.

I am grateful and happy to be able to offer a testimony about **another time in my life when I experienced the genuine joy and success that come from hearing and heeding God's GUIDANCE.** This occurred in October 3rd 2008 when I received a "calling" into the ordained ministry. I did not know what to do. **I heard an inner voice directing me – GUIDING ME --** to share with my pastor, which I did. Because I was a woman, and because I was at 70+ years of age, in a conservative church community, I was wary of how my calling would be received upon its being announced into the membership. There had been and continues to be considerable backlash and resistance against accepting and supporting women as ordained ministers in my denomination of National Baptist Convention, Inc. Despite some pushback and negative responses, though, the membership in general seemed to accept my calling as a valid one.

Now all that remained was the process of ordination. Again, I knew absolutely nothing about this process and what it entailed. Like Dorothy and her friends, I knew that I was in great need of some **GUIDANCE.** I needed a **spiritual GPS ORDINATION App** for 80+ year old black women in a conservative, sexist denomination! What to do? It just so happened that **eight (8) years later**, my brother received and accepted his calling into ordained ministry a few years prior. His experience along with that of my son-in-law (who is also an ordained minister) proved to offer everything I needed to know about the process from preparation to ordination itself. What should not be overlooked here is that BOTH men had been also raised in the denomination, and they had solid knowledge of it. They also knew what resources were available, what pitfalls and personalities to use and which ones to avoid, what formats to adopt, even what days and times to structure the process around. **AND... THEY WERE NOT BITTEN WITH THE BUG OF SEXISM** to the extent that they had any serious diseases of resistance or misogyny.

Then WHAM! **Two (2) years later**, my brother accepted a calling to the pastorate at a local congregation. Again, that **inner voice of Divine GUIDANCE directed me** to join him and his wife and develop under his leadership and help with the ministry. This time, again, **I heard and heeded God's GUIDANCE**. As it would turn out, God was preparing ME as well as the CONGREGATION for the process of my ordination and subsequent ministry. To shorten this story (which is even longer!!) I was ordained at this church with my brother as my Pastor and mentor, the Congregation he served as the supportive church, and my son-in-law as the Chair of my Ordination Committee! **God GUIDED both of them** to plan and implement an ordination process and service that was informative, exciting, and even FUN despite the pressure I felt**! As an 80+ year old black woman I was ordained as a minister in a conservative black Christian denomination on Sunday May 13th, 2018.** Praise God!!!

What a wonderful experience! I am thinking now of all those beautiful, excited, scared, smart, wonderful, ready-to-serve women who were discounted, devalued, discouraged, and denied that opportunity to be ordained. **From Sojourner Truth to Jarena Lee to Minister Carhee to Jean Barnes to Naomi Brown to Bishop Kelly to me… EACH of us (and many, many more women whose names we both know and do not know!)** have experienced and continue to experience the sense of being unwanted, cast out, and forsaken. We have felt that sense of being lost and confused about what to do and where to go after we heard God's call. Like Dorothy and her friends, we were suddenly set in a place that was so new and different that we didn't know what anything meant anymore. **We needed help! We required assistance.** And although we may not have felt it at times, **God – Emmanuel -- was with each of us on our personal journey.** This is how **Divine GUIDANCE** operates. It is **a GPS that GUIDES US** to the most efficient route to success and joy. **God GUIDED** each of us towards an outcome that would reflect God's Will for our lives.

I can still remember one Sunday, over 15 years ago, during a worship experience, the congregation opened our Hymnals and turned

AFFIRMATION #12:

to Martin Luther's moving hymn, **"Guide Me, Oh Thou Great Jehovah"**. On that day, I actually felt chills moving up and down my back, although I didn't understand why. Now I know better. I understand what gains and losses, discovery and uncertainty, clarity and confusion, being lost and finding our way back to the path are all about. **My continuous PRAYER and HOPE today and EACH day** of my life at 83 years is, **"God, GUIDE my life today in all of my thoughts and words and actions."** Faith leads me to believe that God hears and responds positively to my request.

I give thanks and praise to God for the **Divine assistance** God offers to me and EACH of US in every moment of our lives. WHY? Because the **GUIDANCE** that God offers to us is more than a bland offering. Not one of us have to be, nor need to be like those men that were described in Dr. Sapadin's article. Neither do any of us have to be like I was in 2008 during the nation's housing crisis. ALL of us can hear and take heed to Isaiah's liberating words. **WE ALL NEED TO ASK FOR AND SEEK GUIDANCE FROM GOD, ALLOW GOD TO BRING TO US THAT GUIDANCE IN ANY FORMS THAT GOD MAY CHOOSE, AND ACCEPT AND HEED THAT GUIDANCE WHEN IT COMES TO US!!!** I know, without question, that **Everyone Needs Guidance from Time to Time As We Travel the Road Of Life.**

CPSIA information can be obtained
at www.ICGtesting.com
Printed in the USA
BVHW070855120122
625988BV00005B/397